ADVERTISING SPECIALTIES INC.

"We Don't Compete. We Create"

Address: 888 Beaver Grade Road, Moon Township, PA 15108
Phone: 412-262-3720 / 800-475-3340 Fax: 412-262-2668
Email: jradspec@aol.com

JR ADVERTISING SPECIALTIES is not just another Promotional Advertising agency.

JR ADVERTISING SPECIALTIES is a resource for ideas, programs And proven marketing and advertising concepts!

JR ADVERTISING SPECIALTIES

* Will assist in the creation and implementation of programs to:

- INCREASE SALES   - PROMOTE SAFETY
- PROVIDE EMPLOYEE MOTIVATION
          - ASSIST IN REACHING YOUR BUSINESS GOALS

JR ADVERTISING SPECIALTIES

*is NOT just another company selling promotional items!

JR ADVERTISING SPECIALTIES
* IS so much more!!!

Whether you are new to JR ADVERTISING SPECIALTIES or one of our existing clients who has used our services for years, schedule an appointment for us to come in and show you the NEW

JR ADVERTISING SPECIALTIES

What People Are Saying About *Stand Out When You Stand Up:*

Barbara Busey starts with a great title…and it gets better from there! I have worked a lot with Barbara and have learned so much from her. Wonderful speaker. Strong coach. And an outstanding writer. Buy this book. Then, you won't have to sweat the small stuff.

> —Ty Boyd, Professional Speaking and Broadcasting Halls of Fame, Founder of Ty Boyd Executive Learning Systems

This insightful guide is full of practical advice delivered in a wonderfully engaging way. I plan to draw on Barbara's wise counsel—using and re-using this book before any speech I give.

> —Jennie Buckner, retired editor of *The Charlotte Observer*

This book covers everything—and I mean everything, from A to Z—that you could possibly need to know about how to enhance the presentation experience and come across confidently and powerfully. I have seen Barbara's results in our students.

> —Peter C. Browning, Dean, McColl Graduate School of Business, Queens University of Charlotte

Barbara's experience and intuition in making people more competent and confident presenters makes her exceptionally qualified to write a book. An easy, fun and extremely informative read.

> —Ranjana Clark, Executive Vice President, Treasury Services, Wachovia, named one of the "Top Ten Bankers to Watch" in the Carolinas

The ability to present effectively is a crucial business skill. This book tells you how in the most comprehensive and engaging way possible.

> —Thomas M. (Tim) Belk, Jr., Chairman & CEO, Belk, Inc.

Personally, I am today very comfortable as a public speaker. I owe that to the training and coaching Barbara has provided me over the years. Now she brings her wealth of talent to the printed word.

> —Jim Palermo, Executive Vice President, Bank of America, retired

Today's world depends on communication, but the difference between communication and effective communication is the ability to reach out and make a personal connection. Barbara's book provides the fundamentals for such success.

> —David S. Dooley, Executive Vice President,
> R.T. Dooley Construction Company

Stand Out When You Stand Up

An A to Z Guide to Powerful Presentations

Barbara Busey

PRESENTATION DYNAMICS

Charlotte, North Carolina

First printing 2005

ISBN 0-9762239-4-5   LCCN 2004115885

ATTENTION CORPORATIONS, UNIVERSITIES,
COLLEGES, AND PROFESSIONAL ORGANIZATIONS:
Quantity discounts are available on bulk purchases of this book for educational,
gift purposes, or as premiums for increasing magazine subscriptions or renewals.
Special books or book excerpts can also be created to fit specific needs.
For information, please contact Presentation Dynamics,
P.O. Box 11713, Charlotte, NC 28220; 704-527-8258.

To my parents

Robert and Mary Busey,

from whom I received the love and talent
for my profession:

Bob, who was a Toastmaster for many years

Mary, who at age 60 discovered the stage as a comedienne
and has been making audiences laugh ever since

Acknowledgments

I'm deeply grateful to the many people who helped me and encouraged me in my first book-writing venture. My heartfelt thanks go: to Lindsey Boyer and Sue Cohen for masterful initial editing; to my book club members, Lindsey Boyer, Judy Ghoneim, Ellen Pollack, Sherry Smith, and Robin Warren who encouraged me and offered great input; to my friends and speaking colleagues, Angelina Corbet and Emily Huling, whose own forays into the book-writing field inspired me; to Sarah Hoss for her story; to Le Trombetta who offered just one tiny, but powerful piece of advice; to Hilda Gurdian, John Maloney, Yolanda Walton, and Craig Young who generously offered their likenesses for some of the illustrations; to my editor Sue Collier for her insightful mastery of the written word; to all the folks at About Books, Inc.—Debi, Deb, Jennifer, Cathy, Kate—who shepherded me and my book through every step of the publishing process; to all the participants I've taught in my workshops and from whom I continue to learn; and to my family for their love and support and for their reactions to the first glowing editorial evaluation I received:

- My mother Mary: *Would it be okay if I claimed you as a relative???*
- My brother Steve: *Cool! No doubt your years of experience have manifested themselves in a top-notch tome! But…are you sure the reviewer isn't trying to sell you something?* ;-)
- My brother Brian: *WOW! That is fantastic!! Please write my resume for me!! My hobbies are water and snow skiing and marathon running. Did I say WOW!?*
- My sister Sharon: *AWESOME KUDOS! I wish I was there—I'd give you some chocolate.*

Contents

How to minimize it before you speak
How to master it when you're speaking

The three components necessary to be a believable speaker

How to make your content more understandable using the outline form

How to be a more dynamic SPEAKER with your:
  Smile
  Posture
  Eye Communication
  Appearance
  Kinesics
  Expressive Vocals
  Resting Places for Your Hands

The importance of dynamism

How to give and receive feedback for improving your skills

Tips for making a speaking engagement go smoothly

About the Author

Barbara Busey fell in love with the written and spoken word when she was in grade school. At the age of 11, she won the role of Dorothy in the play "The Wizard of Oz." From that point on, she was hooked on the power of the stage and the spoken word. A year later, she submitted an essay to a student contest at the *Akron Beacon Journal* (Ohio). Her first published piece, it won her a $15 prize. And her love of the written word was cemented.

An avid student of communication, she graduated from the University of Georgia with a bachelor's degree in journalism (*cum laude*) and went on to earn her master's in speech communication from Georgia State University.

Today, Barbara has her own business, Presentation Dynamics, located in Charlotte, North Carolina, where she combines her two loves—speaking and writing—into a training and publishing business.

As a trainer and speaker, she specializes in the dynamics of how people present themselves. Since 1990, she has worked all over the country, for clients large and small, from the corporate boardroom to the community classroom, doing workshops and individual coaching to help people from across all types of professions and industries enhance their communication ability.

Her most popular workshops are:
- **The Compelling Speaker**—Presentation Skills
- **Business and Social Dynamics**—Business Etiquette
- **Personality and Team Dynamics**—Myers-Briggs Type Indicator
- **Communic8 Essentials**—Communication Skills
- **Rigorous Writing**—Business Writing Skills

Barbara has trained thousands of business executives and professionals nationwide. Her clients include Bank of America, Belk Stores, Carolinas Healthcare, *The Charlotte Observer*, Coca-Cola Bottling Consolidated, R.T. Dooley Construction, McColl School of Business at Queens University, PricewaterhouseCoopers, Springs Industries, Transamerica Reinsurance, Wachovia, and others.

As a writer and publisher, she has been published in dozens of trade and business publications on communication-related topics. For six years, she was a columnist on "People Skills" in *The Charlotte Business Journal*. Since 2001, she has written the weekly editorial for *La Noticia*, Charlotte's Spanish-language newspaper. (Her communication skills are limited to English, however; she writes for the paper in English and they translate it into Spanish!)

Barbara began her communication career in corporate America. She spent 13 years working in positions such as marketing director and corporate communications director in the retail, real estate services, and financial industries. She also worked part-time during this period as a college instructor in speech communication and journalism courses. Today she serves as an adjunct instructor at the McColl Graduate School of Business at Queens University of Charlotte.

Her skills in written and verbal communication have won her awards from organizations such as the International Association of Business Communicators, the American Advertising Federation, the Public Relations Society of America, and the Association for Women in Communication.

Even in her volunteer activities, Barbara chooses those that are an outlet for her love of communication. She spent seven years as the newsletter editor for a professional women's organization, is currently serving on the speakers bureau for the Shelter for Battered Women, makes a monthly presentation to female inmates at the County Jail on image and esteem issues, and serves as a mentor to a nontraditional woman college student through a scholarship program. She is a member of the prestigious Women Executives and the invitation-only Entrepreneurial Leadership Circle sponsored by the McColl Graduate School of Business at Queens University.

Opening Remarks

Recently I attended a board meeting where we were discussing the presentations and accompanying handouts that were needed at our upcoming annual meeting. At one point, the treasurer quipped, "The thing that's great about having the budget as a handout is I can say, 'As you can see on line such and such…' and everyone's head will go down to look at the item. Then no one is looking at me while I talk!" Everyone laughed. We can all relate to the discomfort of public speaking.

Our Number One Fear

In fact, speaking in public is widely known as humanity's number one fear. To put it in a little perspective, on one famous list of fears, death was ranked number six. It seems people would rather die than give a speech! Why not just let it go at that? If you have a debilitating fear of heights, no way are you going to be convinced to take a walk on the ledge of a 50-story building. So if you're scared of making presentations, why not give them as wide a berth as you do the source of other fears? Why put yourself through the knee-knocking, heart-pounding nightmare of talking before a group?

The Power of Presentations

The answer is simple. It's *power*. Effective presentation skills have undeniable power—the power to help you be more successful, to be more confident, to be more personally fulfilled.

Success is not measured just by how much you accomplish, but rather by how many people know you've accomplished it. If you want to be more successful in your professional and personal life, nothing can give you more bang for your buck than the ability to speak effectively before a group. No other endeavor in your quest for success allows you to reach so many people at once and not only impress them with your knowledge and wisdom, but influence their beliefs and move them to action.

One of my clients, a high-level executive in his company, hired me to help him become more competent and comfortable in his presentations. Claiming this training was crucial to his career track, he said to me, "I *have* to do this." Lo and behold, six months later, this man was named CEO of his organization.

Another client "Rachel," who's an engineer, was petrified of making presentations. She avoided any opportunity to speak before groups. Over time she realized that people quit asking for her input or participation in key meetings. She became frustrated watching others take credit for her ideas and her work, simply because she was too intimidated to speak out. She came to me for training to master her fear and build her skills. Not because she had any desire to rise into the ranks of management, but because she wanted to be more comfortable with presentations. As she said, "I would just enjoy my job more."

A Skill Unlike Any Other

The incredible thing about being an effective presenter is that it can be a transformational experience. Once you

The Rest of Rachel's Story

Rachel's lack of comfort and confidence in speaking stemmed from the fact that when she landed her job seven years earlier, she felt she was in over her head. As a result, she was content to let others present her data for her. But over the years, as she watched her coworkers take credit for her ideas, she knew she had to overcome her

(continued on next page)

2

The Rest of Rachel's Story (continued)

trepidation. That's when she came to me for training.

We did two coaching sessions together with a great deal of videotaping and feedback. Rachel said the videotaping was eye opening: "I didn't look nearly as bad as I thought I did!" That was the shot of confidence she needed. Since her training with me, she is now in charge of a system at her company, which means leading the morning updates every week. The meetings have gone so well and Rachel is so charged with self-assurance that she surprises herself with the conviction she conveys when she has to present controversial or potentially negative information.

In one such case, she told me she was able to influence management to see that the result of one of her department's decisions was not a problem, as some people perceived it, but was in fact a win-win outcome because of a disaster averted. This was a stance she never would have taken without the newfound confidence her speaking skills have provided her.

Last I heard, Rachel has applied for the position of Senior Engineer. She told me that not only would she never have applied for this without the self-confidence her new skills have given her, but, she said, "I know I'm likely to get it because of my belief in myself."

feel the thrill of captivating an audience, of receiving applause and praise, you'll discover an inner power and strength that you've never before experienced. It will give you the confidence to achieve things you never dreamed possible.

As with any other skill, you can build your presentation competence by learning the techniques, practicing, and delivering often. Unlike other skills—say sports, art, or music—you don't have to be born with the talent to become good at it. If you learn the techniques, practice, and speak often, you will build your competence and confidence. You'll stand out when you stand up.

This Book

My primary intent with this book is to help those who make presentations as part of their business or professional life (although there are a couple of chapters devoted to other types of speaking and communication). Whether you present to customers, employees, your boss, a trade group, or a community organization, your effectiveness is important because your credibility is on the line. You want to come across competently and confidently. If you stand out when you stand up, you can open doors of opportunity and possibilities.

How do you "stand out when you stand up"? *You have a compelling message that you deliver with energy and confidence.*

How do you learn the techniques to achieve that? Ideally, practicing in front of a video camera with a coach is the best way to master your skills. But if you don't have that opportunity, then this book will help. It's loaded with practical, specific techniques and guidelines from A to Z that can diminish your nervousness, improve your effectiveness, and increase your confidence.

Read it and leap—into a new world of opportunity!

A

Anxiety

I went to stand up at the podium and my mind sat back down.

—JIM ROHN

If you're a breathing, feeling human being, you'd be a rare breed if you've never experienced any of these gut-wrenching symptoms of public speaking: butterflies in the stomach, dry mouth, sweating palms, racing heartbeat, quivering voice, twitching muscles, breathlessness, nausea. Maybe you've panicked and drawn a complete blank; maybe you've frozen or broken out in tears or passed out cold. There probably isn't a person alive who has not endured some kind of speaking jitters.

Speaking in public is the number one fear. So if you've ever been in the grips of that debilitating fear, you can take some comfort in the fact that you're not alone. In fact, you're in excellent company. Sir Laurence Olivier suffered from it. Helen Hayes battled it. Barbra Streisand and Carly Simon have been incapacitated by it. Winston Churchill fainted dead away from it.

What Are We Afraid Of?

What is it about standing in front of a group of people to talk that so completely unnerves us? There are a couple of things going on. One is the fear of failure. However, believe it or not, I think this is a minor fear. Let's face it. We all fail at things during the course of our lives—heck, even during the course of our day. Failure can be disappointing,

Churchill's Collapse

Winston Churchill was making his second speech ever before the House of Commons. In his first one, he'd spoken of his experiences in the Boer War and he did fairly well.

So he wasn't prepared for the overwhelming fear that gripped him that second time. Like many speakers, he was worried that he wouldn't have enough to say, so he chose a wide range of issues to discuss—taxes, education, foreign policy. But it was too much for a single speech, and overwhelmed by the difficulty of addressing so much complexity at once, he collapsed in the middle of his talk.

Churchill went on to become one of the greatest speakers ever known in the English language. Entirely self-taught, he mastered a stutter, a lisp, and debilitating fear to lead not only a nation, but the world, with his masterful oratory skills.

but unless you're a die-hard, obsessive perfectionist, it's generally not debilitating.

I think there's another fear underneath all this—the fear of *making a fool of ourselves.* You've probably never given this phobia much thought. But think about how much it operates in our daily life: It affects how we dress for that party, how we behave with the boss, how we interact with a client. Most of us are sensitive to the conditioning of our civilized society and want to behave in ways that won't embarrass us.

When we stand before an audience—with several sets of eyes trained on us—we feel vulnerable. We are keenly sensitive to the fact that we don't want to appear foolish. We want to project poise and confidence, but are afraid we're going to look and sound like a blubbering idiot no one will take seriously. It can potentially be a very public way to humiliate ourselves. Hence, our panic.

It's worth it to get a handle on this because the rewards of handling yourself well in front of an audience—being poised, dynamic, and unflappable under pressure—are immeasurable. Virtually everyone I've trained will admit that once they can get past the fear, they experience an incredible rush. There is nothing quite like the thrill and power of captivating an audience and having them hang on your every word. And as I address in Chapter Y—You, there's nothing more important to success than the exposure public speaking can bring.

So let's look at the two avenues for dealing with the fear: how to be less nervous in the first place, and when you are experiencing it, how to get a grip on it and overcome it.

Minimizing the Anxiety

There are several things you can do to reduce your anxiety before you speak. I've captured them all with "P" words.

The 7 Ps:

1. **P**repare. It's extremely risky to believe that you can show up for your talk and just wing it. For starters, you need to know your subject matter. And you should do your homework to find out who your audience is (see Chapter K—Knowledge). Preparation also means planning and organizing your talk. Develop it in a concise, bullet-point outline form so you can easily refer to it to keep your train of thought without reading it verbatim (see Chapter C—Content). Lack of preparation increases the odds that you'll lose your train of thought, draw a blank, or ramble aimlessly—all anxiety-ridden experiences.

2. **Plan to use P**rops or visual aids. This tip may have you scratching your head. But I'm going to introduce a concept here that I'll refer to again and again in this book: *purposeful movement.* I believe this is one of the secrets of being a compelling speaker. When all your movement is purposeful, it gives you more power. Using a prop or visual (see Chapter V—Visual Aids) is a great form of purposeful movement. It gives you something to do with your hands, something to focus on. This in turn can diminish the helplessness that often comes with anxiety. Since you're usually the most nervous at the beginning of a talk, starting with a prop or visual will give you more of a sense of control and purpose. An added benefit of visuals is that they can serve as your notes, which will also reduce your anxiety.

3. **P**icture **your success.** Visualize yourself giving a dynamic, well-received presentation. Just as expecting the worst can be self-fulfilling,

so can anticipating success. When you rehearse your presentation, visualize yourself appearing calm, cool, and collected while giving an outstanding, well-received presentation—and it will be more likely to actually happen that way.

4. **Be (more than) Punctual.** Arriving just in the nick of time means you're going to be harried and distracted. Ideally, arrive early enough to give yourself plenty of time to set up, get focused, and learn the lay of the land. Get a feel for the layout of the room, where you'll be standing, where the screen is, how the equipment works. Don't be afraid to rearrange some chairs, the lectern, or the screen to make it easier for you. A little reconnaissance can go a long way toward making you feel comfortable in the room.

5. **Polyester-proof yourself.** This may sound crazy, but your clothing is crucial. If you know that you tend to get flushed and hot when you're nervous, don't wear heavy or tight-fitting garments. Make sure you wear clothing that breathes. Polyesters and other manmade fabrics don't breathe. That means when your body's temperature rises from your anxiety, the heat can't escape. Polyester clothing gives new meaning to the term "sweating it." Choose natural fabrics— cotton, wool, silk, linen—for optimum breathing ability. Ladies, if your fair complexion tends to blush when you're nervous, especially on the neck and upper chest area, avoid scooped neck blouses. High collars or turtlenecks do a good job of camouflaging one of the most flush-sensitive parts of the body.

6. **Practice makes perfect.** Rehearse aloud in front of your mirror or a video camera or another person. Reading it to yourself doesn't count. The more you deliver it aloud, hearing and feeling the words roll off your tongue, the more familiar you'll be with it and the more comfortable you'll be when it's time to give it.

7. **Present often.** Instead of ducking opportunities to speak, seek them out. Like any skill, you will get better at it and more comfortable the more often you do it.

Managing and Mastering the Anxiety

Okay, you've tried all those preparation tips to minimize the nerves, but there you are up in front of the room and suddenly that little knot of anxiety becomes a full-blown noose. It's hard to breathe, it's hard to think. Now what? Here are two categories of remedies for dealing with the anxiety when you're feeling it.

Physical Techniques:

1. **Move!** Physical movement can be a great help in reducing nervousness. This is because nervous energy is generated by adrenaline—that old "fight or flight" chemical. Fighting or taking flight is movement. But think about it. What do most of us do when we're nervous? We clam up. *Must remain calm. Don't show any nervousness.* If you mistakenly try to hold it all in, if you don't exert some physical movement, then all that nervous energy is going to manifest itself in all sorts of unpleasant ways. The next thing you know, those butterflies have turned into barracudas. When you exert yourself, you're giving that nervous energy something to do, besides eating a hole in your stomach!

Before you speak, do some isometric exercises: Push against a wall; try to lift up your chair while you're sitting in it; press your palms together and release; do neck rolls; tighten and release different muscles.

During your talk, don't stand rigid, hiding behind and gripping the lectern. Stride across the front of the room. Use big, purposeful gestures. Put energy in your vocals—vary your volume, rate, and inflection. Physical movement not only keeps your anxiety from overcoming you, but also gives the added benefit of making you look more dynamic and compelling (see Chapter D—Delivery).

2. **Pause.** This is an invaluable speaking technique. Don't be afraid of a little dead air. A pause allows you to collect your thoughts when they've suddenly evaporated. It makes the audience anticipate what you're going to say next. It's an opportunity to take a sip of water. It helps you vary the rate of your talk and keeps your pace from getting too fast. It gives you the opportunity to breathe.

3. **Breathe.** This is one of the most important things you can do. Think about all those symptoms I listed at the beginning of this chapter. Virtually all of them are exacerbated by lack of oxygen. The human body needs oxygen during times of stress. Your lungs, your heart, your muscles, even your brain cells crave it. Yet when we're nervous, most of us tend to breathe shallowly, depriving ourselves of that life-giving force. So before you speak, take deep, slow breaths. Whenever you feel on the edge of panic during your presentation, pause—and take a deep breath. You'll be amazed at how much better you'll feel if you'll just do some deep, conscious breathing.

Mental Techniques:

1. **Adjust your attitude.** Instead of being me-focused—*Oh no, I'm so nervous. I'm going to make a fool of myself. No one will like me. No one will listen to me.*—try to be genuinely audience-focused. Think about what you have to offer them, what fantastic pearls of information they're going to learn, what unique insights they're going to walk away with, what good decisions they'll be able to make because of your great information. Think about what you can do for *them*, not what they're doing to *you*.

2. **Lighten up.** Try not to take yourself too seriously. Have fun. Learn to laugh at yourself. So what if it's not perfect? It won't kill you, honestly.

Anxiety

As a professional speaker and trainer, I've spoken thousands of times. You can be assured that I've encountered just about every type of presentation glitch there is. I've had every known type of audio/visual equipment fail on me at some time or another. I've had no A/V equipment available when it was promised. I've had the power go out in a windowless room. I've shown up without my handouts. I've lost my voice at the start of a presentation. I've spoken in rooms with terrible lighting, dreadful acoustics, horrible seating arrangements. You name it.

But I learned years ago to say to myself, *So what?* That attitude can take you a long way toward putting things in perspective. This is not a life-or-death situation. You will survive. Besides, it gives you some great stories to tell later.

Additional Help with the Speaking Jitters
Do:

- Have a glass or bottle of cool water handy. It helps with dry mouth, plus gives you something to do when you need to pause to collect your thoughts.
- Break up a lozenge into tiny pieces and suck on the slivers. This is a great

Skirting Anxiety

By far, my most memorable public speaking moment was when I lost my skirt! It was during a business etiquette workshop. I was wearing a beautiful purple suit. The jacket was long, coming to about mid-thigh, with several buttons up the front of it. The skirt was a wrap-around style. From one button on the right, it wrapped around to another button on the left, with a diagonal scalloped edge down the front.

As I was beginning my presentation, this thought went through my head: *Gee, it sure did get drafty in here all of a sudden.* I soon realized that the button on the left side was gone; I looked down to see that my skirt was hanging wide open. The only thing saving me from total indecency was my long jacket.

Can you picture it? My legs are sticking out from under my jacket, and I'm sporting a purple tail! Was I embarrassed, mortified? You better believe it. But I said to myself, "Okay, Barbara, practice what you preach—*so what?*"

(continued on next page)

Skirting Anxiety (continued)

I looked up at the group and cried, "How long were you going to let me stand up here like this?!" There was a wave of relieved laughter in the room. After asking if anyone had a safety pin, I took one proffered by one of the participants, pinned my skirt back together, and went on with the program.

The fact that I didn't make a big deal out of it meant that the audience didn't make a big deal of it. The rest of the workshop went great. You've got to learn to lighten up.

device for generating some moisture in a dry mouth and the tiny pieces can be sucked on discreetly and unobtrusively.

- Put Vaseline on your teeth for dry mouth. It prevents the feeling that your lips are stuck together.
- Have a great opening. It builds your confidence and creates momentum.

Don't:

- Drink anything cold or with ice. Cold temperatures contract the vocal chords.
- Eat or drink any dairy products beforehand. Dairy can have a constricting effect on breathing and vocals.
- Memorize your speech. This creates even more anxiety when you forget what you're supposed to say.

Remember, speaking in public is like any skill. Keep in mind this well-known model of the four stages of learning a skill:

1. **Unconscious incompetence—** We don't know that we don't know.	3. **Conscious competence—** We are aware of gaining skill.
2. **Conscious incompetence—** We know that we don't know.	4. **Unconscious competence—** We don't have to think about our skill.

Many people never get past Stage 1 because they've never taken the time to learn their strengths and weaknesses and how they could get better. Ironically, many of these speakers may have developed a comfort level because they give a lot of presentations. But that doesn't mean they're good!

Many others never get past Stage 2 because of the fear. But if they'd just hang in there, they would find themselves beginning to transition into the last two stages easily and naturally.

So to master your anxiety, you first have to learn the tricks of the trade. That may actually increase your anxiety somewhat as you move into Stage 2, since you become self-conscious about everything you haven't mastered. But the second key is to keep on doing it. That is the only way you'll move through stages 3 and 4. Believe me, Stage 4 is a satisfying and gratifying place to be.

B

Believability

I'm glad this term comes at the beginning of the alphabet and therefore the beginning of this book. Because believability is the cornerstone of all communication. Why? Well, think about it. You may have the solution to my problem, the answer to my need, the best invention since the computer chip. But if I don't *believe* that you do, then it doesn't matter, does it? I'll never give you the chance to prove it. So believability—or credibility—is essential to our success in life. And as a presenter, the impact of your message will be significantly determined by how believable you are.

Believability is composed of three elements:

1. **Competence.** This refers to your experience, knowledge, or expertise. This is not necessarily about being an educated professional. If I have a noise in my car's engine and ask two people about its cause—a car mechanic and a nuclear physicist who has never so much as looked under the hood of a car—whose diagnosis will I be more likely to believe?

2. **Trustworthiness.** Obviously, I'm more likely to believe you if you have a proven track record of being honest and reliable and doing what you say you'll do.

3. **Dynamism.** When you project energy and enthusiasm, it conveys to people that you have confidence, that you believe in yourself.

14

Believability

Audiences are going to have a hard time being motivated by you if you don't have conviction and passion for what you're saying.

As a speaker, it's certainly important for you to possess knowledge about your subject (competence) and have a reputation of being honest and reliable (trustworthiness). But here's the rub. You may possess those two characteristics and still not be *perceived* as believable, because you lack that third element—dynamism. Without a doubt, the single most important quality you can convey as a speaker is energy. Audiences will forgive a lot if you bring passion to your subject. But the most interesting information in the world will be lost on an audience if it's delivered in a dull, boring, apathetic manner.

The secret to conveying that dynamism lies in the three elements of communication:

1. **Verbal**—what we say
2. **Vocal**—how we sound
3. **Nonverbal**—what we look like

Research done by sociolinguist Albert Mehrabian revealed that only *7* percent of our communication impact comes from our *verbal* message, the actual content of what we have to say. But *38* percent of the impact comes from our *vocal* qualities— tone, rate, inflection. And over half, *55* percent, comes from the *nonverbal*—our facial expressions, body language, and other nonverbal qualities.

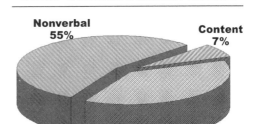

YOUR COMMUNICATION IMPACT

It's not that *what you say* doesn't matter. But *how you say it* and *what you look like* when you say it will determine how your message is received. So a presentation delivered in a ho-hum monotone and listless manner is not going to get your audience excited about your message. Vocal and physical energy is what makes a speaker compelling—and believable (see Chapter E—Energy).

C

Content

Begin at the beginning and go on till you come to the end, then stop.
—LEWIS CARROLL,
Alice in Wonderland

Although research says our verbal content is worth only 7 percent of the impact of our communication, it doesn't mean your content isn't important. It's just that how you look and sound determines how your message is interpreted. If your delivery (see Chapter D—Delivery) is powerful and dynamic, and if you possess competence and trustworthiness, then audiences will be hanging on your every word. So it makes sense to ensure that your content is understandable and interesting.

In this chapter, we're going to look at the elements that make content *understandable*. We'll cover the guidelines for making it more *interesting* in Chapter H—Humanizing elements.

Preparation

If you've ever experienced any of these dilemmas in preparing a presentation, it's a good sign that you might be in trouble:

- You're trying to prepare a speech and you have no idea where to begin.
- It all comes easily to you as you're preparing, but you discover the talk is three times longer than the time you've been allotted.
- Despite the fact that you make extensive notes on everything you want to say, during the presentation you find yourself rambling

or you draw a blank and can't seem to pick up the thread of your thoughts.

- It takes you forever to prepare a speech because you revise it over and over. Then when it's time to deliver it, you feel panicked and confused because you just can't keep straight what you wanted to say.
- You write out every single word and end up reading the speech verbatim.

These dilemmas are all symptoms of poor preparation. And it's in the preparation that we're going to create an understandable presentation.

For an audience to understand your message, it must:

- Have a clear purpose.
- Be aligned with the audience.
- Not run over the time frame allotted.
- Be organized in a logical way that's easy to follow.

In order to fulfill these criteria and create an understandable message, there are two steps:

Step 1: Get Everything Down PAT

Purpose. What do you want to accomplish? Are you providing information? Showing the solution to a problem? Proving a fact? Do you desire to create action, change behavior, or influence opinion? You must be clear on what your objective is so that you can get the desired result from the audience.

Audience. Who is your audience? What is their knowledge of, interest in, and attitude toward the topic? Toward you? Are they more likely to be big picture- or bottom-line-oriented? Or will they want to know all the details? Failure to understand and relate to your audience can derail an otherwise great presentation. For example, if you were a gardening expert, can you imagine how self-defeating it would be if you gave the same presentation on gardening to a group of botanists, a sixth grade class, and some homeowners who wanted to learn how to start a garden? The audience will determine how you approach your topic, so invest time in gaining some insight into who will be sitting in that room listening to you.

Time limit. How much time do you have? By far, the most common error I see in presentations is the speaker trying to cram in more information than time will allow. Honoring time limits is the mark of a well-prepared and respectful speaker. Think of all the times you've been in an audience—or on the agenda—when a speaker or series of speakers all went over their allotted time. Audiences get antsy and start to tune out. It throws off the agenda of an event where several presentations are scheduled. It leaves the impression that the speaker didn't care enough to plan ahead, that he doesn't respect the audience members' time. Keep in mind, though, that the shorter your talk needs to be, the more preparation time you'll need.

> **Woodrow Wilson** was once asked how long he took to prepare a speech. "It depends on how long it is," he replied. "For a 10-minute talk, I need about two weeks. For a 30-minute talk, I need about a week. For an hour-long speech, I'm ready right now."

Once you know what you want to accomplish, who your audience is, and how much time you have, you're prepared for the second step.

Step 2: Organize Your Talk with the Outline Form

The outline form, presented in the box to the right, is the simplest, yet most powerful, tool for organizing and delivering your thoughts in a way that's logical and cohesive—in other words, understandable.

At the end of this chapter, there's an example of a speech outlined with this form.

Preparation Tip

Before I explain each of the elements of the outline, let me share a good preparation tip. When preparing your talk, tackle the body first. Identify the main points you want to address. You can't come up with an at-

> I. Introduction
>   A. Hook
>   B. Reason to listen
> II. Body
>   A. Road map
>   B. Main points
>   1.
>   2.
>   3.
> III. Conclusion
>   A. Summary
>   B. Close

tention-getting opener or a powerful close if you don't know what you're going to say. So the first step is to identify the key points you want to address. Three to five points is usually the most manageable number. Then develop each point with explanations, examples, and evidence. This is why it's important to know how much time you're going to have. You can expand or condense the information for each main point depending on how long your presentation needs to be. So if you come up with five main points, then for a half-hour talk, you can spend about five minutes apiece on them. But if you've been asked to give a 15-minute talk, you know you're going to have to cut it down to less than three minutes per point.

It's important to identify the main ideas that you always want to get across, whether it's a 10-minute talk or a two-hour presentation. Learn to edit or expand on the supporting information so you never have to sacrifice any of the major ideas. One of the most common speeches I give is on tips for good delivery skills. As you'll see in the next chapter, I've come up with the acronym SPEAKER that covers the seven key tips for being a more dynamic speaker. I've given that talk in anywhere from 20 minutes to an hour. Obviously, the less time I have, the more editing I have to do, leaving out some examples and anecdotes. But the important thing is, I will always get my seven tips in.

Only after your main points are fleshed out should you go to work on the introduction and conclusion.

The Outline

Now let's look at each of the elements of an outline. Think about a huge, Dagwood-like sandwich. The top and bottom slices hold the sandwich together and contain a little relish and condiments for taste and interest. But the bulk of the sandwich is all the meat and goodies in between. That's a great analogy to the outline form. The Introduction and Conclusion are brief, adding interest and holding the whole talk together. But the meat of the presentation is in the middle, the Body of the talk.

Introduction

Your introduction has several purposes. It sets the stage; it establishes your credibility and rapport with the audience; it gets your momentum going; it makes the audience want to listen to you. The two elements in the introduction help achieve these purposes.

Hook. First you want to get the audience's attention. A great hook will make the audience take notice and want to listen to you. Please note, a good hook is not: *Good morning, my name is _____ and today I'm going to talk about....* Ho hum. I'm not saying you shouldn't introduce yourself if necessary, but don't start out with that. Engage your audience. Intrigue them. After you've reeled them in and gotten their complete attention, then it makes sense to introduce yourself.

Possible hooks include:

- A startling statement or statistic: *Every 10 seconds. That's how often a woman is battered by her partner in this country.*
- A story or anecdote: *When I was a child, my grandfather took me fishing every weekend....*
- A prop or visual aid: This can be a great way to start not only because it can be engaging but also because it gives you something *purposeful* to do. Having something to do with your hands, something to focus on, can help you get focused and centered and allay your anxiety (see Chapter V—Visual Aids).

Examples of Hooks

The publisher of a Spanish language newspaper:
Buenos días, Amigos. Como están? Yo estoy contenta de estar aquí hoy. How many of you understood what I just said? Not many of you, I see. The reason I started in Spanish is to help you understand a little how it feels to be a foreigner trying to understand a different language. What I said was: "Good morning, friends. How are you? I am happy to be here today."

A business consultant on the importance of having a business plan: All of you have traveled before, right? You arrive at the airport, pull up to curbside baggage check, and the skycap jumps over to help you with your bags. And what's the first question he asks? "Where are you going?" What if you said, "Well, gee, I don't know. You pick."

A child advocate: "I'm going to read a quote from a 16-year-old boy that was printed in the paper recently." Reading from a newspaper clipping, she said, "'You feel like you're on top of the

(continued on next page)

20

Examples of Hooks (continued)

world. You can do whatever you want to do.'" Then she asked, "Considering the source is a teenage boy, what are some of the things you might think he would be talking about?" Responses from the audience included driving a sports car, an athletic achievement, a kiss, good grades, getting his driver's license, drugs. After the responses seemed to taper off, she said somberly, "He was talking about the thrill of holding a gun in his hands."

- A question: *How many of you are parents?* or *Have you ever wished you could see into the future?*

Just a little tip here. When you ask a question that you want a response to, make sure you word it so that you do, in fact, get a response. Suppose you ask, *Is there anyone here who doesn't like ice cream?* First of all, starting with "is" implies a yes or no response, not a show of hands. Second, the use of the negative makes it confusing. It could have a rhetorical meaning—*Imagine anyone not liking that dairy delight*—which doesn't call for a response. It could also mean you want to know *Who dislikes ice cream?* In that case, a few hands might go up, which could dilute your impact if you plan to praise the virtues of ice cream. So word your question in a way that will get a significant response: *How many of you like ice cream?*

- A quote: *Thomas Edison said that genius is 1 percent inspiration and 99 percent perspiration.*

You may have noticed I didn't include telling a joke. I talk about this more in Chapter J—Jokes. A joke is a highly risky way to open a talk. If it bombs or offends someone, you have a lot to overcome. It's safer not to open with a joke. That doesn't mean humor isn't appropriate. A humorous story or anecdote that happened to you personally can be a very effective opening.

It's important that your opening be *relevant* to your subject. It serves no purpose to ask your audience if they've ever vacationed in the Caribbean, then proceed with a talk that has nothing to do with tropical paradise.

A strong opening ensures a great start. It establishes your momentum and helps diminish your anxiety. You should never shortchange a good hook.

Reason to listen. How will the audience benefit from your talk? How will it will make them happier, safer, more successful, make their jobs easier, make their wallets thicker? What credibility do you have to speak to them on this topic? You want to set this up early in your talk so your audience will be more motivated to listen to you.

Body

Now we get to the meat of your talk. Here is where you present your main ideas in a logical order and explain and elaborate on each point as much as your time limit allows.

Road map. Just as a map on a road trip helps you know where you're going, a road map for your talk lets the audience know where you're going to take them. It makes it easier for them to follow along. This is the same thing as the classic speech adage, "Tell 'em what you're going to tell 'em." It doesn't have to be long and involved. You don't even have to—and shouldn't!—give away your points up front. Simply saying, *This morning I'm going to explain the three strategies behind our new marketing plan,* tells your audience your topic and lets them know you're going to cover three main points. Anytime you can quantify your main points—*I'm going to talk about the five most docile breeds of dogs—* it makes it easier for your audience to follow.

Main points. There are several ways you could order your ideas. You'll probably find that your subject lends itself easily to one of these common formats:

- Topical—Your main points are arranged by particular topics. In a presentation on public speaking, the topics I could organize my talk around might be anxiety, content, and delivery.
- Chronological—Your main points follow a natural sequential flow. If, for example, you were explaining a cookie recipe, you would start by talking about the ingredients you would need and then work your way through the process of mixing the dough and baking the cookies.
- Spatial—Your points are arranged according to geography, such as reports about the north, south, east, and west divisions; or a description of a room, building, or city.

- Problem-solution—This is just what it sounds like. You first explain the problem you encountered, then describe how you solved (or propose to solve) it.
- Past-present-future—Although similar to a chronological ordering, this one is less about a series of steps and more about generalities over a time continuum. This is common in presentations about the state of a company. The speaker might first praise the company's past accomplishments and its triumph over early struggles. Then he might talk about where it is today in size, sales, product line, and so forth. Finally he would look toward the future, where he sees the company headed over the next few years.

A talk with a persuasive purpose, where you want the audience to take action or believe something, requires some special organization techniques, which are discussed in Chapter S—Selling.

A final tip about ordering your main points: Whenever possible, make it easy for both you and your audience by using some kind of memory device, like the examples below. It makes you less reliant on notes and gives the audience a way to follow along and remember your points.

- Alliteration—the 7 Cs of Communication (Confidence, Components, Competence, Credibility, Clarity, Caring, Convincing)
- Acronym—SPEAKER
- Alphabetical—such as the way this book is organized

Conclusion

The ending of your talk is important because it's your last chance to make a good impression. It's often what the audience is most likely to remember. To be effective, it should comprise two things: a summary and a memorable close. Notice, however, how I've inserted the Q&A session.

The **summary** is where you bring it all home, wrap it all up, deliver one final gem that embodies the essence of what you've said. *So, in order to get this project started, we need a budget of $100,000 and a team of four people who can be dedicated to it full-time.*

Open for Q&A. In order to preserve the impact of your close and end in a way that's meaningful and memorable, consider opening the floor for questions *before* you deliver your closing (see Chapter Q— Questions): *Before I close, are there any questions?* This prevents struggling to find a way to end your presentation after Q&A: *Well, if there aren't any more questions…then, um, I guess that's all.* Save your closing for after your Q&A session, so your powerful conclusion isn't weakened by questions that follow.

The **closing** brings the talk to a definitive and memorable end. You can use the same tools in closing as in your hook: an anecdote, story, prop or visual, or quotation. *Benjamin Franklin said, "Well begun is half done." If you will approve the allocation of these resources, our project will be halfway completed!*

A Final Thought About Creating Your Outline:

Don't write out your presentation word for word. Use key words and bullet points—enough to keep you on track, but not so much that you feel the need to read them. The outline allows you to be conversational, a compelling attribute of a great speaker.

Content

Sample of a Speech Outline

This is the outline of a speech I occasionally give on Domestic Violence. Notice the use of key words and phrases except for the statistics I needed to read.

I. Introduction
A. Hook: How many of you know someone who has been a victim of DV?
   Tell story of my friend who was murdered by her husband.
B. Reason To Listen: DV is problem for society: (read stats)
   • One in four women are battered regularly.
   • Four women a day are killed by their partners.
   • Domestic violence is the single major cause of injury to women—more women are beaten than are raped, mugged, or in accidents.
   • 25% of all pregnant women experience battering, causing more birth defects than all other illnesses and diseases combined.
   • U.S. businesses lose $3 to $5 billion each year because of abuse-related absenteeism, and $100 million in related medical costs.
   • 90% of all female inmates have been battered.
   • Cost of support services to victims, law enforcement and the court system: inestimable.

II. Body
A. Road map: What, Why, How to help, the Shelter
B. Main points
   1. Definition of DV
      Power and Control Wheel—the ways men abuse women:
      Physical, emotional (intimidation), isolation, financial, sexual, children, blame, male privilege.
   2. Why does she stay?
      Hope—cycle of violence: honeymoon always follows incident.
      Fear, love, guilt, shame, economics, would I be believed, religion.
   3. What can you do?
      Volunteer, donate, hotline, legal support, court escort, use your expertise, financial, safe homes network.
      Take victim seriously, be concerned, get her to safe place, encourage her to leave, don't blame her, don't make decisions for her. Refer to shelter.
   4. Shelter Services

III. Conclusion
A. Summary: Why this issue is so important
   [Q&A]
B. Close: Read poem: "I Got Flowers Today"

D

Delivery

When I was in college, I had to take a biology course. It was held in one of those large auditoriums that probably sat 300 people. In every class, the Einstein-looking professor delivered the day's lecture by reading from a three-ring binder in a dull monotone. He never looked up at us, never varied his droning voice. He never moved from the lectern except to turn his back on us and scribble some complicated formula on the blackboard. Countless students dozed off during his lectures. I sat there, bored stiff, trying to pay attention and taking notes as best I could. I'm embarrassed to admit that Biology 101 was the only course in my life in which I received a "D." While I can't blame it entirely on the professor—science was never my best subject—I have no doubt that if he had been a more dynamic and engaging presenter, I might have learned a little more.

Remember Mehrabian's breakdown of the verbal, vocal, and non-verbal? Only 7 percent of the impact of our communication comes from *what we say*. The other 93 percent comes from *the way we look and sound* when we say it. This is what delivery is all about—how we use our vocal and nonverbal qualities to present a message that's dynamic and compelling. It's a fact: The most important meaty content is worthless if it's delivered in a boring, monotone manner. But if your delivery is dynamic and engaging, audiences will hang on your every word.

The secret to being a compelling speaker is in the delivery. There are seven key skills to being a dynamic speaker, which I have summarized with the acronym SPEAKER.

Smile.
When you're speaking, what is the audience looking at? Your face, of course. So smile at your audience. Let them know you're pleased to be there. How many times have you seen a speaker whose face was frozen in a mask, not moving a single facial muscle? He didn't look happy to be there, did he?

If you have a serious topic or bad news to deliver, I'm not suggesting that you need to grin like the Cheshire cat. But let your facials be expressive. If

> ## Smile How-to Tip:
> Think to yourself, "I'm happy to be here; I'm happy to share this information with my audience." Then tell your face!

you're speaking of something that makes you angry—or concerned or confused—let your face show it. You have a lot of muscles in your face, so use them.

Have you ever heard the old saying, "It takes more muscles to frown than it does to smile"? Well, I'm not sure I believe that. Think about it. A smile has to work against gravity—that takes a little effort. So be conscious of it—smile. The added benefit of this is that when you smile at your audience, they will smile back. That will go a long way toward helping you get comfortable and build your confidence.

Posture.
Your stance in front of a room says a lot about how comfortable and confident you appear. Picture a woman standing with all her weight on her right leg, her right hand grasping her left elbow, her left foot grinding the floor like she was putting out a cigarette. Or how about this? A man standing with his left foot crossed over to the other side of his right foot, slouching with his hands shoved in his pockets. Neither conjures up an image of someone self-assured and confident, does it?

> ## Posture How-to Tip:
> Envision a pole running from floor to ceiling right through your spine. Like a bumper car attached to a metal rod, you can move all around, but you can't slouch or lean on one leg.

A balanced stance has a lot of power. Distribute your weight evenly on both feet. Stand tall, don't slouch. Pull your shoulders back; lift your chin up. This is not to imply ramrod-straight military posture. Just make sure your rib cage is lifted. Good posture will give you a more poised and confident appearance.

Keep in mind that you don't have to plant your feet like they were nailed to the floor. Movement is good. You can stride from side to side, or from the lectern to your screen. The key here is *purposeful* movement, not pacing or rocking or swaying, or what I call "nervous dance steps." One way to ensure this is to take at least two steps in any direction. If you take just one, it's not purposeful.

Another Posture How-to Tip:

Having a problem with dance steps? Try putting a coin in one or both shoes to remind yourself to plant your feet.

This is a good place to address a common practice of some speakers: walking out into the audience. It is purposeful movement and can make the speaker feel more connected to the audience. But I urge caution at making a habit of this for three reasons:

1. First of all, what seats in a room are taken first? The ones in the back, right? For whatever reason, people often prefer to sit the farthest distance from the front of the room. They did not choose to be close to the speaker, so I hesitate to encroach on those invisible boundaries they set up.

2. Second, when you walk deep into an audience, it means that those in the front will have to turn around to see you. You are making it more difficult for some members of the audience to see you.

3. Third, when those in front do turn around to look at you, what are they seeing? The back of you. I never deliberately present my backside to an audience. Not only is it rude to turn your back on someone, but I never know what my backside looks like!

Eye Communication.
Notice I didn't say eye *contact*. You can make eye *contact* with people by glancing up occasionally as you read from your notes or from your visual. But eye *communication* implies that you're connecting with your audience. To truly make an impact on your audience, you need to make members feel like you've looked at and talked directly to each of them individually.

Here's a checklist of eye communication **Don'ts** that, when violated, will diminish your power:

- Don't read your speech, rarely glancing up.
- Don't pretend to look at the audience by looking over their heads.
- Don't dart your eyes around the room, never really focusing on anyone.
- Don't exclude someone from your eye contact when the group is small.
- Don't appear to look at the same person to the exclusion of others.
- Don't look at the visual more than your audience.
- Don't look down at the floor or up at the ceiling, or anywhere but at the faces in the crowd.

Eye Communication How-to Tip:

As you look at individual audience members, pretend each one is the only person in the room, that you're having a one-on-one conversation with him or her.

Look 'em in the eye. Talk *to* them, not *at* them. An added benefit of good eye communication is that it can also help with nervousness. If you imagine that you're simply having a conversation with one person at a time, it helps you get over the anxiety of speaking to a whole group.

The greatest gift you can give as a speaker is to make each audience member feel like you're talking to him. This means you need to hold a person's gaze for a few seconds. Look at each person individually and briefly talk to her and no one else. For a relatively small group, say a dozen or less, it shouldn't be difficult at all to engage every single person. For mid-sized groups of 20 or so, it might be a little more difficult, but still doable. If you're speaking to a large audience, say a hundred people or more, you can't possibly connect with every single person. So don't try. Instead, concentrate on engaging as many as you can, ideally in different parts of the room.

Appearance. When you're in front of a room, does your appearance command attention, give you credibility, imbue you with power? Or is it weak, sloppy, uncertain? How you appear to your audience has an impact on your believability and how receptive they'll be to your message. There are actually two subsets under the "appearance" category that I'd like to address: attire and distracting mannerisms.

Attire

This is not a "dress for success" lecture, but there are a few things worth mentioning when it comes to what you wear for a presentation.

Looking good. In today's business casual world, the traditional business suit is far less common than it used to be. But just because business casual has become the predominant dress code, it doesn't mean the standards of neatness, good fit, and appropriateness should be ignored. You still want to look your best in order to project a credible image.

When you're standing in front of a group with several sets of eyes focused on you, it's not the time to wear the pants that are a little too snug, the panty hose with a run in it, or the shoes that haven't been polished. You want to look your best, which means garments that are clean and pressed and fit you well. Also consider what clothing makes you look good. In other words, you may have a great outfit that looked good on the rack, but if it doesn't make *you* look good, it's not enhancing your appearance. For example, a double-breasted suit can be sharp, but it doesn't look nearly as good on a short, portly gentleman as it does on someone who's tall and broad-shouldered.

Fabric choices. If you tend to get hot when you're nervous, don't wear heavy material. Make sure you wear a fabric that breathes. Polyesters and other manmade fabrics do not breathe and will make you sweat all the more. Stick with natural fabrics—cotton, wool, silk. But be careful of choosing something like linen, which wrinkles.

Appropriateness. Consider what's appropriate for the audience and the occasion. Certainly, if you were presenting to the board of directors, you wouldn't think of showing up in a casual outfit. But if your audience is more informal, you could seriously separate yourself from them if you showed up dressed to the nines. A good rule of thumb is to dress one notch above your audience. So if your audience is a group of construction workers in jeans and flannel shirts, you might want to consider khakis and a golf shirt. If your audience is dressed in a standard business casual, a notch above that for men would be a sport coat over a tieless shirt; for women it might be nice pants and a jacket.

Keep this rule in mind—the more skin that's exposed, the more casual the look. Therefore, short sleeves are more casual than long sleeves, a sleeveless top is more casual than short sleeves. A short skirt is more casual than a long one. Sandals are more casual than shoes. A scooped or plunging neckline is more casual than a conservative collar. Even in your casual attire wardrobe, you can still make choices that are more professional than others.

Color. Most men have that charcoal gray or navy blue suit for their best look; women often choose black as their power color. But the fact is that many of us don't look good in those colors. If you choose a color that's complimentary to your skin tone and hair and eye color—either warm tones or cool tones—you'll find that you'll look better. Poor color choices can wash you out, which is not the kind of appearance you want to have in front of a group.

> ### *Color Tip:*
>
> Keep in mind that whenever you wear two contrasting colors—such as dark pants with a light shirt—you are essentially cutting yourself in half. This creates the illusion of a shorter, wider figure. If you want to cut a taller, more slender figure, then choose the monochrome look—a top that matches the pants or skirt in color.

Distracting Mannerisms

Have you ever seen a speaker do or say something that absolutely drove you to distraction? I'm thinking about things like jingling change in his pocket, or playing with her hair, or saying "um" every few seconds. If you want an appearance that's poised and credible in front of an audience, be aware of and monitor any of those little pesky traits that serve no purpose except to drive an audience crazy. Remember, movement that's purposeful has power. A distracting mannerism refers to any movement that's *not* purposeful. Let's look at three categories of distracting mannerisms:

1. First is anything you put in your hands. It's true a prop is something that gives you purposeful movement. If you held up a globe to point out a location in Asia, that would be purposeful. But if you didn't put it down afterward, and just started idly spinning it on its axis while you were talking, that would no longer be purposeful, just distracting.

There are many sources of distraction that we can hold in our hands. I've seen speakers repeatedly click a pen, uncap and recap a magic marker countless times, unfold and refold a paper clip over and over, twist and turn and fold and bend their notes (which they never looked at), and fiddle with the cordless mouse so much that their PowerPoint advanced several slides without their awareness. None of these actions is purposeful, and the end result is an appearance that projects anxiety and lack of confidence. The best rule of thumb is, unless you have a specific, purposeful use for an object, keep things out of your hands. That way, you won't be tempted to play with them.

2. The second category of distracting mannerisms is, well, ourselves. This includes playing with your hair, fingering a button, twisting a ring, playing with jewelry, tugging at your cuffs, stroking a beard, readjusting your tie, shoving glasses up your nose. I'm not saying that if you need to brush a lock of hair out of your eyes or if your tie needs straightening, you shouldn't do it. But when those kinds of movements are repetitive, they serve no purpose—except to distract.

3. The final category of distracting mannerisms is, actually, vocal. *You know, haven't you, um, ever heard, uh, a speaker who, you know, while he spoke, he, um, couldn't seem to, ah, get through a sentence, you know, without, um, filling it with nonwords?*

There are many names for these little vocal monsters: nonwords, fillers, vocalized pauses, word whiskers, vocal tics. These words have no meaning—they're not purposeful. The common culprits are: *um, uh, you know, like, really, okay, right, basically.* But it could be anything. I've heard speakers whose fillers were whole sentences. One that comes to mind is a man who ended virtually every sentence with, "Ya know what I mean?" Once I was in an audience listening to a speaker whose nervous tic was clearing his throat. Ahem, I swear, ahem, he did it, ahem, after every three, ahem, or four words. After the speech,

Vocal How-to Tip:

To minimize nonword fillers, try rehearsing your talk aloud with *your teeth clenched*. You'll be amazed at how much those pesky fillers will diminish.

several members of the audience who knew what I did for a living came up to me to let me know how many "ahems" they counted! In other words, they weren't listening to what he said. His vocal tic was too distracting.

The thing about distracting mannerisms is that they are just that—distracting. They detract from what we have to say and usually make us look nervous and uncomfortable. The best way I know to avoid these nasty image-detractors is to be videotaped. Only when you see yourself as others do can you really appreciate how you might be sabotaging your presence in front of an audience.

Do not underestimate the power of wearing the right attire and minimizing those distracting mannerisms when it comes to exuding a confident, powerful appearance.

K̲inesics.

This may not be a familiar word to you, but you've probably come across its cousin, "kinetics." Kinetics is the science of motion, as in physics—what goes up must come down. Kinesics is the science of body motion and how it communicates. So, for example, if I respond to your question with a shrug of my shoulders, I've communicated to you without speaking, haven't I? If someone winks at you across a room, there's communication going on. A nod or a headshake is a form of kinesics. When you point to convey directions, or use your hands to show an object's dimensions, or hold up fingers to represent a number—those are all examples of kinesics.

As a speaker, you want to use kinesics. Physical movement and gestures will help make you a more powerful speaker. Once again, we get back to that key word—purposeful. A repetitive gesture is not purposeful and will become

Kinesics How-to Tip:

Think "purposeful." Can you envision a gesture that would go along with these phrases?

"It could fit in the palm of my hand."

"This is important to me."

"You are the key to our success."

"There are three important points here."

"As you can see here on the visual..."

The more your movement is descriptive and purposeful, the more natural and dynamic you will look.

33

a distracting mannerism. Purposeful gestures seem to naturally accompany what you're saying.

Purposeful gestures can also be implicit. Think about the bold, underline, and italics features in your word processing program. Your gestures can do that as well. They can highlight what you're saying and add emphasis the same way your word processing features do.

Gestures give meaning and power to your presentation. I've often had workshop participants worry that they used their hands too much when they talked. But the truth is, I've never seen "too much." As long as they're purposeful, gestures will enhance your presentation, not detract from it.

Expressive Vocals. Have you ever heard someone speak who had absolutely no movement in his voice? IF-IT-COULD-BE-PLOT-TED-ON-A-GRAPH-IT'D-COME-OUT-AS-A-STRAIGHT-LINE-WITH-NO-VARIATION-IN-IT.-HOW-DO-WE-TEND-TO-RESPOND-TO-PEOPLE-WHO-TALK-LIKE-THIS-FOR-VERY-LONG?... Zzzzzz... The *monotone* is deadly dull. If you want to be engaging and keep your audience's attention, then you must have interesting vocals.

Among your many vocal elements, pitch is the one thing you don't have much control over. Some of us have high-pitched voices, while others are deep baritones. You can't change that without straining your vocals. But just about everything else you can modulate.

Volume. You can speak loudly and get the audience's attention. Or it can be just as attention-getting if you drop to little more than a whisper. However, just as you wouldn't want me shouting at you all during my speech, neither would you stay tuned in if I murmured throughout it. The key is *variety*.

Beware of the dropsies. This is when people let their voices trail off at the end of their sentences. They start out strong, but just seem to run out of steam. Sometimes, people's voices drop off so much that you lose what they're saying. So make sure you project strongly through the end of each sentence.

Rate. Think about little kids. What happens to their rate when they get really excited about something? *Mommy,mommy, lookat thisneatrock Ifound!* Enthusiasm naturally translates into an increased rate. But on

34

the flip side, sometimes it's engaging to slow down…pause…let your last point sink in…or let your audience anticipate…your next word. Once again, the key is variety—vary your rate to lend interest.

Tone. Tone is the style or manner in which you speak that expresses emotion. Since I can't very well give an example of tone of voice here, I'll simply refer to the old saying: "You catch more flies with honey than you do with vinegar." Your tone of voice is what determines that sweet or sharp attitude.

> **Expressive Vocals How-to Tip:**
> Try *smiling* while you're talking—it's a great way to ensure that your tone will be pleasant.

Inflection. The other vocal element that's crucial to being an interesting speaker is the opposite of the monotone—inflection. Inflection is purposeful and meaningful emphasis on words. Inflection is to your vocals what gestures are to your nonverbals—it gives meaning and power. Let's look at an example of the impact of inflection.

Barbara didn't finish the report today.

Try speaking the sentence aloud several times, each time emphasizing the highlighted word:

Barbara didn't finish the report today. (Someone else did.)

Barbara *didn't* finish the report today. (She didn't get the task done.)

Barbara didn't *finish* the report today. (She started it, but…)

Barbara didn't finish the *report* today. (Maybe the letter, but not the report)

Barbara didn't finish the report *today.* (Maybe yesterday, maybe tomorrow)

Look at all the different meanings conveyed by changing the emphasis. This is what inflection can do. It gives your voice color and richness and helps you communicate your meaning.

Let me mention a particular inflection problem. When we ask a question, our inflection naturally goes up at the end of the question. *Is it time to go?* But when we use that upward inflection at the end of a declarative sentence, it makes us sound tentative and unsure. *This report covers every aspect you need to know? The committee made their decision?* A downward inflection at the end of every sentence will convey more certainty.

Conversational. The key to natural vocal delivery is to be conversational. A speaker who reads verbatim from a script is helping no one but insomniacs. Memorizing a speech can also prevent a conversational style because it more than likely sounds forced and insincere. (Memorization is not a great speaking technique. Not only may you sound artificial, but it can wreak havoc on your self-control if you forget what you're going to say next.) The key to being conversational is to know your subject and then outline your main ideas in key words and phrases. Then you can use your notes as speaking points. This allows you to talk to your audience in a natural style, which will be more engaging and interesting.

Resting Places for Your Hands. Your hands convey a lot about how comfortable and confident you appear. You want to use purposeful gestures, but, of course, that doesn't mean you're gesturing all the time. I've also recommended that you keep things out of your hands. So, what do you do with your hands when you're not gesturing and you can't hold on to anything for security? How you hold your hands when they're "at rest" can be called **resting places** or **home bases**.

Resting Places to Avoid

Before I give you descriptions of the most powerful and confident resting places you can use, let's look at those that are *less effective* so you can eliminate them from your repertoire.

1. **Hands in the pockets.** While this does not necessarily look bad, particularly on men, the problem is that it's so comfortable, you'll inevitably end up with your hands shoved in there too long. You'll

have no kinesics—you lose that energy and movement that are so crucial to a dynamic presentation.

2. **Crossed arms.** This can be comfortable, but in body language, it sends a signal of being closed or defensive. Not the kind of message you want to send to your audience.

3. **Hands on the hips.** This can be construed as arrogant—"I'm in charge here and you're not." Not the attitude you want to convey.

4. **The arm clutch.** I've dubbed this the "book report" position, because to me it looks just like I felt that first time in grammar school when I had to stand up and give a book report. I was nervous, frightened, and felt like I was hanging on for dear life. One arm reaches across the front of the body to clutch at the elbow of the other arm—or the upper arm or forearm or even wrist. Another variation is to reach behind your back to grab the other arm. Can you see how pained and uncomfortable this posture appears? Again, not the image you want to present as a speaker.

5. **The fig leaf.** If the term doesn't help you visualize this, then picture the arms hanging down in front of your body, with the hands loosely clasped together in front of the groin area. In and of itself, the fig leaf is not such a bad thing. It is a respectful posture. It would be a very appropriate stance when, say, the flag is going by, or the national anthem is being played, or someone has asked for a moment of silence. By being respectful, though, this posture is also *deferential*—it *defers* power away from you. As a speaker, you don't want to defer that power—you want to own it and project it. So the fig leaf is not a good choice to achieve that.

Effective Resting Places

If you want to appear confident and comfortable when you're making a presentation, the following positions make the *most effective* home bases.

1. **Arms at your side.** If you let your arms hang loosely down at your sides, it can be an appropriate resting place. However, I have a caveat here. I've seen some people stand like this with comfort and ease. I've seen others who looked like they just grew their arms today and haven't yet figured out how to deal with them. It's too unique to each person to be a universal rule. But I can tell you this. If, when you stand with your arms hanging at your side, you feel awkward or uncomfortable—guess what? That's how you're going to look. So you're just going to have to try it and be the judge. If it feels comfortable on you, it'll undoubtedly look that way.

2. **Parade rest.** This is where you clasp your hands behind your back. Some people call it the "reverse fig leaf." This is a powerful posture—it pulls your chin out, pulls your shoulders back and lifts your rib cage. It gives you a good, confident stance. However, I'm going to put a big qualifier on this one, too. Because it looks so good and is also comfortable, the tendency is to lock into it and never come out of it. There goes your kinesics, your purposeful movement. So here's my recommendation. Save parade rest for when you're *not* talking. When you're taking questions or comments from the audience, parade rest makes a great listening pose. That's really its best use.

38

3. **Arms up.** This position calls for you to bend your elbows at a right angle and place your hands loosely together in front of your solar plexus. The 90-degree angle is key, because if it's any wider, it lowers your hands and becomes a fig leaf. If it's any tighter, it raises your hands, which can look like you're praying. I know, I know—sometimes that's what you feel like doing, right? *Please deliver me from this presentation.* But it's not the confident look you want.

What's key about how your hands come together in this position is that they are relaxed, not tense.

Examples of relaxed include:
- Interlacing your fingers
- Cupping one hand around the other
- Placing one hand in the other
- Steepling your fingertips together
- Lightly touching your knuckles together

Examples of tensed include:
- Gripping your hands
- Twiddling your thumbs
- Twisting a ring
- Cracking your knuckles
- Wringing your hands
- Doing isometrics with your fingers

This arms-up position combines power and confidence. By holding your arms up at that right angle, you are exerting energy and therefore projecting power. And by bringing your hands together in a relaxed—not tense—manner, you appear confident and at ease. The other advantage to this home base is that you're already halfway to a gesture. To me, it just seems to naturally lend itself to gestures and kinesics—a good thing.

4. **One-arm up.** Picture the last home base I just described with both arms bent at right angles. Now, drop one arm to your side and keep the other at that 90-degree position. The arm that's up should have the hand loosely closed, not clenched or splayed open (or tucked into your jacket a la Napoleon!). To visualize this, picture yourself standing around talking at a cocktail party, holding a drink in one of your hands. The placement of your arm and hand in that situation is virtually the same for the one-arm up position.

For a subtle variation of this home base, you could place your other hand in your pocket. That can project a confident, polished look (providing, of course, that it doesn't stay buried in there and comes up for air once in a while!). Just like with both arms up, the one-arm up balances energy and power with ease and relaxation—a powerful combination for a speaker to project.

I don't want to imply that the rest of this book has no value, but if there's one chapter that's more important than all the others, this would be it. Remember, 93 percent of your communication impact comes not from what you say, but how you look and sound when you say it. If your delivery falls flat, the greatest content in the world will be meaningless, because you won't be able to engage your audience.

E

Energy

Remember the three elements of credibility? Competence, trustworthiness, and *dynamism*. Dynamism is crucial for a speaker. I've mentioned the significance of energy before (see chapters B—Believability and D—Delivery), but it's so important that it deserves its own chapter. As a speaker, you must project energy and enthusiasm.

It's not unusual in my workshops for some participants to claim that they are just not demonstrative by nature. They feel uncomfortable—unnatural—when they have to turn on all that extra energy. My challenge is, first, to show them that just because it *feels* unnatural doesn't mean it *looks* that way, and second, dynamism is not only attention-getting and credibility-building, but it simply makes the speaker more compelling.

I have a favorite exercise I love to do in my classes. I start a story and tell the participants that they're to take turns picking up the thread of the story and continuing it. The rules are simple: They can forget everything they learned about organization—in fact, the story doesn't even have to make sense; and they can forget all the delivery tips—no need to worry about posture, eye communication, home bases, and so forth. There's only one requirement. They must push their energy level way outside their comfort zone—big gestures, exaggerated vocals. In other words, they must feel like an idiot.

41

The results of this exercise are amazing. Everyone agrees afterward that they *felt* ridiculous. But when we watch the video playback together, everyone agrees that no one *looks* ridiculous. In fact, it was evident that the energy made the story more fun, more humorous, more engaging.

It doesn't matter whether you think it's in your nature or not. If you want to be a dynamic speaker, you've got to push your energy beyond your everyday level. The reasoning behind this is what I call "the goldfish bowl syndrome." Picture a goldfish swimming around and around in its bowl. While he's exerting his normal energy level for his little world, you probably wouldn't find it interesting to watch him for long, would you? Think about what that fish would have to do to keep your attention. Bug his eyes out? Blow bubbles? Do back flips out of the water? You would undoubtedly find these activities more engaging. Yet that poor fish would definitely be outside his comfort zone.

When you're speaking before an audience, you're like that fish in the bowl with the audience looking in. If you exert your normal energy level, you'll be about as exciting as the goldfish. You've got to get outside your comfort zone physically if you want to keep your audience's attention and interest.

You project energy through expressive vocals and purposeful gestures and movement. Vary those vocals. Stride across the front of the room. Use big, descriptive gestures. This is the secret to standing out when you stand up. And there's a bonus. The more energy you use, the less nervous you'll be. As I said in Chapter A—Anxiety, nervous energy is really the "fight or flight" chemical adrenaline. It needs to be released, otherwise it's just going to wreak havoc on your body. Projecting all that energy will free you from the grip of anxiety. It's so powerful.

F

Feedback

In my workshops, every participant receives extensive feedback and coaching on his or her presentations. This critiquing is done not just by me, but by the others in the class as well. I give participants this opportunity to be "coaches" for several reasons. By paying attention to other speakers' skills, it makes people more sensitive to their own skill set. By practicing the art of positive, constructive feedback, participants are honing a skill that will be invaluable to them in their working life. And by learning to be open and receptive to all kinds of feedback, a speaker can receive new insights into how to make an even stronger impact.

The objective of effective feedback is to achieve a positive change in behavior without hard feelings or resentment. Being a good coach will help you be a good speaker. Being open to coaching will help you become even better. Here are some keys to effectively giving and receiving feedback.

Giving Feedback:

- Be specific.

  Not: *Great job!*

  Instead: *You were very well organized and delivered with great enthusiasm.*

43

- Focus on the issues, not the person.

  Not: *You didn't do a very good job of choosing your topic.*

  Instead: *I'm not sure that subject was appropriate for this audience.*

- Look at specific **presentation** elements: the opening, the close, the visuals, and so forth.

  —*I didn't hear a reason to listen.*

  —*I wasn't clear on what you were trying to persuade me to do.*

  —*The visuals were just right—not too many, just enough to complement your talk.*

  —*The transitions didn't seem strong to me, so I got lost a couple of times.*

  —*You did a great job with that tough, emotionally charged question—not letting it rattle you and answering it factually.*

- Look at specific **speaker** factors: eye communication, gestures, nonwords, and so forth.

  —*I didn't feel like I got much eye communication from you.*

  —*There were several times where it was hard to understand you, perhaps because you were mumbling or just not projecting as much as you should.*

  —*You had such balanced posture and natural gestures, you didn't look nervous at all.*

- Frame your comments in the context of *not* what the speaker's doing "wrong" or "bad," but how she can get "even better."

  Not: *You said way too many ums.*

  Instead: *If you could minimize the ums, it would make you sound more confident and sure of yourself.*

- Monitor purely subjective comments—be prepared to explain yourself in objective terms.

  Not: *I thought it was good.*

  Instead: *I felt it was good because you took a technical, complex subject and made it clear and understandable to this audience.*

  Not: *You came across poorly.*

  Instead: *You didn't come across as well as you could have because you read straight from your notes—as a result, your voice was fairly monotone and you didn't have any eye contact with the audience.*

- Offer as much (or more) positive feedback as constructive comments.

Receiving Feedback:

- Be open-minded and receptive.
- Take the attitude that this information is designed to help you, not attack you.
- Listen objectively and resist defensive reactions.
- One of the best ways to determine the validity of feedback is to get yourself videotaped. This allows you to see and hear yourself as others do, which will make the feedback make more sense.
- Analyze the criticism and decide whether it's valid or not. Keep in mind that you don't have to do anything that's recommended to you if you feel that it's unfair or inapplicable. But remember that if you hear a similar refrain over and over, it's probably an area that you need to address.

G

Gigs

So you've been asked to speak somewhere. It might be an industry trade meeting, a church group, any civic, professional, community, or nonprofit organization. But if it's outside your normal work environment, it's bound to create a little extra stress. Here are some tips to help make a speaking gig go smoothly.

Have a Contact

There should be someone—a meeting planner, the program chair, the organization president—who will serve as your contact for this speaking engagement. Use this person's knowledge of the organization, the meeting, the audience, and the facility to help you prepare for the presentation. It's helpful to have one point person who can help coordinate all your needs, such as audio/visual equipment, microphone, directions to the meeting, and hotel accommodations if necessary. You want to have someone to contact should you encounter any problems.

Know the Audience

Find out who will be in the audience. A presentation on nuclear energy to a group of grade school students would be entirely different than to a group of homeowners who lived near a nuclear power facility. What is the audience's knowledge of and attitude toward your subject? Are they likely to be interested in and favorable toward your topic? Or could they be apathetic or even hostile? The more you know about the audience, the better you can structure your approach to meet their needs.

Know Your Time Limit

This is an often-violated guideline in presentations. If your contact says you have 30 minutes to speak, *including Q&A*, make sure your talk is less than half an hour so there will be time for questions. Review the information in Chapter C—Content as a reminder of the importance of knowing your main points, then editing or elaborating on them according to how much time you have.

When you rehearse your talk, time it so that it's roughly 70 percent of the time you've been allotted. If you've been given 20 minutes, your rehearsal should last 14 to15 minutes. There are several advantages to this. First of all, it's not at all unusual, once you get your stride and find yourself enjoying the presentation, to succumb to the temptation to stray a little during the presentation. You'll be reminded of a great story or a perfect example that you'll suddenly be compelled to share. The 70 percent rule gives you the cushion to do that. This cushion also allows for any questions or comments that might be interjected during the talk. Finally, if you don't go over your original rehearsed time, you'll be a hero to your audience. Read between the lines on this: Audiences will always forgive you for going *under* your time limit.

Ask for What You Want

If you've been asked to speak at a large conference or trade meeting, you may well deal with a professional meeting planner who will know all the right questions to ask you. But most of your small professional and civic organizations are run by volunteers. A program chair may have very little idea of what a speaker might need. You need to be clear and forthright in your requests. Just stating that you're planning on using a PowerPoint presentation may result in disaster if you assume the organization will provide the equipment, but your contact believes you will.

So ask for what you want. Here are some considerations to factor into your requests:

- What is the size of the audience? If it's large, say over 50, then a microphone will undoubtedly be necessary. Ask for a lavaliere mike (see Chapter M—Microphone). If that's not available, then find out exactly what the PA system will be.

- Are you planning to use any audio/visual aids? If you want a flip chart and markers, ask for them. Need a TV/VCR to show a video? Request it. If you're going to be using PowerPoint, ask for a computer projector. If you're not going to be bringing your own laptop to hook up to the projector, inquire whether a laptop can be provided. Be sure to find out whether it takes a diskette or CD.

- What room logistics do you prefer? Do you want a lectern, a table, or nothing at all in the front of the room? Where would you like the screen located—in the center or angled off in a corner? Do you need a chair up front? Would you like to have water handy? What kind of seating would be best for your presentation? If there is flexibility on the seating, indicate whether you'd like it arranged in auditorium style (rows of chairs), in a U-shape, or whether you'd like the audience sitting at tables either classroom style or at rounds. To avoid as much last-minute rearranging as possible, you could send your contact a room layout diagram indicating the placement of everything the way you'd like it.

- Do you want to provide handouts? Ask the meeting contact if the organization will make the appropriate number of copies from your original—most of them will happily comply. If it's a large group and the organization is unable to make copies, then ask if they'll reimburse you for the expense of making the copies yourself.

Get There Early

Arrange to arrive for your presentation early. This gives you a chance to check out the room and make any adjustments to the room set-up or equipment. It gives you time to do something as simple as moving the lectern from one side to the other. Perhaps you want to change the location of the screen. Maybe you'd like to rearrange the chairs. Recognize that you have a right to make the room as conducive to an effective presentation as possible.

If you're using a PowerPoint slide show, you absolutely want to get there early enough to check all the equipment and make sure you know how everything works. Whenever I'm communicating with my meeting contact, I always ask if he or she is knowledgeable about the A/V technology. If so, I ask if that person can arrive early to help me. If, however, my contact is not savvy in that area, then I ask if there's a computer or A/V technician available who can be there when I arrive.

Remember, if an organization has invited you to speak, it's for a reason. They might want to learn more about your job, your company, or your area of expertise. Accept this honor graciously. Never apologize for your self-perception of ignorance or inability. *I don't know why you wanted me to speak. I'm really not a very good speaker. This really isn't my area of expertise. There are certainly others who know more about this than I do.*

While your purpose with such statements may be to ensure that the audience won't have high expectations, what they really do is set you up for failure in the audience's eyes. *Gee, he's right—he's not very good. I'm sure someone else could have told us more.* Even if you feel unqualified (which, of course, you never should; see Chapter K—Knowledge), even if you're worried about making a fool of yourself, don't let your audience know. Deliver with energy and confidence. If members of the audience enjoy themselves during your presentation, they will forgive—and probably not even notice—your apprehensions.

For more information on how to generate speaking gigs for yourself, see Chapter Y—You.

H

Humanizing

Undoubtedly, you've heard more than your share of speakers who delivered a dry, fact-loaded speech. I've got nothing against facts, mind you. But if all you do in your presentation is recite a laundry list of facts, figures, and statistics, why are you there? Just give me the report, for crying out loud, and I'll read it for myself.

If your delivery is dynamic and compelling, then audiences want to hear what you have to say (Chapter D—Delivery). If you used the outline form to organize your talk, then it will be understandable to your audience (Chapter C—Content). But is it *interesting*?

What makes content interesting and memorable? Not facts, statistics, numbers, or raw data. The audience wants your take on the information, your spin, your interpretation. What's the story behind the numbers? What does your information mean for your audience? As a speaker, you have an opportunity to make your information real for the audience. You can do this by *humanizing* the talk.

Humanizing your presentation makes it meaningful and memorable. It shows you have a grasp of the issues, and it makes it interesting for your audience. There is probably no other device that can create such a powerful connection with your listeners. If you want your audience focused, tuned in, and mesmerized, then humanizing your content will do the trick. Here are some examples of humanizing elements.

Involve the Audience

Don't just talk at your audience—involve them in your presentation. Ask them questions, conduct exercises, do a survey, break out into discussion groups, reward them for participation with little giveaways. People absorb information better if they're involved in it.

Use a Prop

I've seen speakers use fruit, an umbrella, a cupcake, a baseball mitt, a cup and saucer, a yoga mat—just to name a few—all to great effect. Once an environmentalist used an apple to represent our earth. Little by little, she cut off and discarded pieces of it, describing how each piece represented the oceans, inhospitable land, developed areas. What she finally had left was 1/32 of the apple. She peeled the skin off that tiny slice. "This tiny bit of peel represents the thin surface of the earth's crust, which is less than five feet deep, upon which we grow the food to feed the world." (See Chapter V—Visuals for more information on props.)

Giveaway Gimmicks

• I know a trainer who starts every workshop with a fistful of dollar bills. She gives one to the first person who answers each of her questions. It's clever and exciting, albeit a little expensive!

• I have a supply of pencils with the words "You are great" engraved on them. I occasionally use them as rewards for participation or as prizes for some type of contest we do in the workshop.

• Candy is a popular giveaway. One of the most creative forms is the gold foil-covered chocolate coins.

Make an Analogy

This is a powerful way to give numbers meaning. Once I heard a college president compare the population of the world to the number of people in the room, which was about a hundred. She cited many world facts in this context, such as "66 of you would be non-Christian; 70 of you would be nonwhite; 80 of you would live in substandard housing; 50 of you would suffer from malnutrition." She pointed to one table and said, "The six of you own half the wealth in this room—you six are Americans…" She concluded by saying, "And only one of you would have a college degree."

Tell a Story or Anecdote

A diversity expert, speaking on the need to accept people's differences if we are to embrace diversity, told a story of the elephant and the giraffe. The gist of the story was that the giraffe felt rather smug because he had invited the elephant to come in out of the cold to live in his home. Yet the elephant was unhappy because he didn't "fit" the narrow doorways, steep stairwells, and high windows. The giraffe's magnanimous solution was to tell the elephant to go on a diet and to exercise to stretch his legs and neck. The speaker made the point that this was often the mistaken way we deal with diversity in our organizations.

True-life anecdotes are also powerful. There was the urban minister who spoke about his youth ministry. Despite the impressive numbers and statistics he cited indicating the success of his work, what the audience remembered was his story about being mugged on a New York street, talking to the mugger, and holding the troubled youth as he cried in the minister's arms.

Use a Visual Aid

A picture is worth a thousand words. And I'm not talking just about photos. One of PowerPoint's greatest values is its ability to convert numbers or percentages or trends into a chart or graph. Anytime you can put numbers into a picture form, you make them instantly more meaningful to the audience. Remember the Mehrabian percentages I talked about in Chapter B—Believability? In a presentation, I could simply state those numbers:

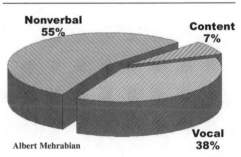

YOUR COMMUNICATION IMPACT

Nonverbal 55%

Content 7%

Vocal 38%

Albert Mehrabian

content—7 percent; vocal—38 percent; nonverbal—55 percent. But the visual impact when they're portrayed in a pie chart is so much more memorable. Use visuals to "pictorialize" your data (see Chapter V—Visuals).

Use Humor

A joke can be a great tool—*if* you're a good joke teller, *if* the joke is funny, and *if* it's not offensive. That's a lot of *ifs* to overcome (see Chapter J—Jokes). The safer and usually far more effective technique is to relate a personal humorous anecdote. I remember a salesman who was talking about the importance of never assuming the customer understood. He related a story about the time his toddler son had an earache. The doctor prescribed a liquid medicine because it was easier for an infant to take than a pill. "When it came time to administer the dose," said the speaker, "I poured the measured amount into a small cup. My son insisted that he be allowed to take the medicine himself. So, proud of his bravery, I handed him the cup. And he promptly poured it into his ear…"

Give an Example

That, of course, is what I've been doing throughout this chapter. Giving an example gives your point meaning and brings it to life.

Recognize that you can make even the driest subject much more interesting if you add humanizing elements.

I

Introductions

An introduction is a form of a presentation. The introducer's job is to make the speaker sound interesting and fascinating, someone the audience just can't wait to hear. When an introducer can make the speaker look good, that in turn will make the introducer look good.

Guidelines for Preparing and Delivering an Introduction

- Resist winging it or relying on memory. Get information from your speaker ahead of time, either from a bio or through an informal interview. Then draft your remarks—in bullet points—and talk from them.
- A good introduction essentially includes three elements:
  1. The speaker's name. Make sure you know how to pronounce it correctly.
  2. The speaker's credentials. Avoid reading his life history—select only the information that's *relevant* to the audience and the occasion. For example, if you're introducing a world-class mountain climber to your outdoor adventure group, a detailed history of his 15-year career as an accountant is not going to be relevant. If, however, you were introducing that same speaker

54

to a group of CPAs to talk about tax laws, that career history would indeed be relevant while his mountain climbing experience would be less germane.

3. The speaker's topic and its importance to the audience. A good introducer will let the audience know how this speaker's information can be helpful to them.

- An optional element is anything that the speaker and audience have in common, such as shared values or goals, organization membership, common struggles, similar background. This is helpful in creating a bond between the speaker and the audience. I once spoke to an organization called the Association for Women in Communication (AWC). Years earlier, I had not only been a member of one of its chapters but had been its president. That created a link I had in common with the group, and my introducer included that information in her introduction of me.

- Keep it brief but complimentary. An introduction shouldn't be a speech. On the other hand, don't insult the speaker by providing just some cursory remarks: *Here's Sandy Banks, an accountant, who will talk to us about the new tax laws.*

- Don't steal the speaker's thunder or try to outshine the speaker. Just because the speaker is known as a great wit doesn't mean you have to do your own stand-up comedy routine. If the speaker is an expert in some area, there's no need for you to impress the audience with your knowledge of the subject. Resist the urge to add your own insights or thoughts on the speaker's topic. This is the speaker's time to shine; your job is to simply make him look good.

- Humanize the speaker—say something interesting and personal about her, don't just recite a laundry list of accomplishments. Ideally, this is something beyond *She's married and has 2.3 kids.* If you know the speaker, you might be able to speak to some personal trait you admire about her or re-

Humanizing the Speaker

One time a banking executive introduced me to a small group of managers I was going to be training. After he talked about my credentials and the reason this training was so important, he said,

(continued on next page)

Humanizing . . . (continued)

"Now, Barbara recently told me that she's getting ready to celebrate one of those 'big' birthdays. In honor of the occasion, she's renting a villa in the Caribbean and inviting several of her friends to join her for a week. I understand that she hasn't yet finalized exactly who's going with her."

Then he smiled mischievously, looked around at the group meaningfully and said, "Maybe if we play our cards right, we could be Barbara's new best friends."

That was a great humanizing element.

late an anecdote that's humorous or characteristic of her positive traits. If you don't know her, then make sure you have a conversation with her ahead of time to see if you can learn something interesting about her.

- Resist clichés: *Without further ado...* or *A speaker who needs no introduction...*

Instead use: *It gives me great pleasure to present...* or *Please join me in welcoming...*

- As you're talking about the speaker, resist looking at and talking to him during the introduction. Talk to the audience, not the speaker.
- After you've made the introduction, stay at the lectern until the speaker reaches your side. Greet her with a handshake and smile and turn the stage over to her.

Suggestions for When You Are the Speaker Being Introduced

- Give your introducer *all* the information and *only* the information you'd like used in your introduction. Avoid handing over your resume.
- Prepare your introduction the way you'd like it used and ask the introducer to present it that way.
- Appear interested and attentive during your introduction: Don't study your fingernails or seem to be engrossed in your notes.
- Resist thanking the introducer for that *wonderful* introduction. Say thanks, but keep it simple.

The Speaker Who Needs No Introduction

One of my clients, David Dooley of R.T. Dooley Construction, once asked me to help him with the remarks he was going to make at an important dinner his company was hosting. He was responsible for introducing the guest speaker at the event, Retired U.S. Navy Commander Scott Waddle. Waddle had been the commander of a U.S. submarine that had a fatal collision with a Japanese fishing boat in 2001. My client had sent every single guest a copy of Waddle's book (*Doing the Right Thing*) in advance. He'd also placed a copy of the commander's bio at every place setting at dinner.

I suggested to David that he not repeat all the biographical information the audience already knew but instead create a moving, humanizing introduction that would make the speaker look good and make the audience want to listen to him. These are the remarks we crafted:

"It is my pleasure to introduce our speaker tonight, Retired U.S. Navy Commander Scott Waddle. As I get older and grayer, I have come to realize that life is like one giant classroom. Each day brings new experiences that can serve as great lessons. If we're lucky, we can learn from those lessons and become wiser and more productive. Tonight is one of those occasions when we can learn valuable lessons from someone else's experience.

"I gave all of you a copy of Scott's book. Whether you've read it or not, you're undoubtedly familiar with the event that occurred three years ago off the coast of Hawaii when a nuclear submarine performed a surface maneuver that resulted in a collision with a Japanese fishing vessel. Nine civilians were killed. Scott Waddle was the commander of that submarine, the *USS Greeneville.* Unlike many other leaders in the public eye who have denied or made excuses for their behavior, Scott stood boldly and took complete responsibility for the accident. His story is an inspiration to all of us who strive to do the right thing.

"Ladies and Gentlemen, please join me in welcoming Scott Waddle..."

This moving introduction brought the audience to their feet for a standing ovation before Scott Waddle even began speaking!

J

Jokes

A colleague once told me about his attempt to tell a joke to a large industry meeting. To ensure that it would go over well, he decided to try it out on the president of the group the evening before. After dinner and, I might add, a couple of drinks, Dave told his joke. The president laughed uproariously. He was holding his sides, unable to contain his mirth. Dave was thrilled his joke had gone over so well and couldn't wait to tell it in his presentation. So the next morning, Dave stood before the group of a couple hundred people and opened with his joke. Nothing happened. The audience was dead silent. Not even a titter. Dave was mortified. It threw him so badly, he ended up stammering just a few disjointed remarks and sitting down almost immediately.

Dave's experience was a perfect example of why jokes are so risky. If your joke-telling bombs, for whatever reason, it's an extremely difficult situation to overcome. It's much harder to go on as if nothing was amiss when you're feeling embarrassed and humiliated because you didn't get the laugh you expected.

Yes, some speakers tell jokes quite effectively. A joke can be a great humanizing element *if* it's funny, *if* people "get it," *if* you can tell a joke, and *if* it doesn't offend someone. Those are a lot of "*ifs.*" For that reason, I don't recommend telling jokes unless you have a solid track record of being funny. Even then, it's a huge gamble.

58

But this doesn't mean you need to forgo humor. It's important to distinguish between being funny and having a sense of humor. A sense of humor means being able to look at things from an offbeat angle, perceiving relationships others might not see. It means being able to laugh at yourself. And that usually means getting an appreciative response from your audience.

Ronald Reagan is a famous example of someone who had a sense of humor and incorporated it into his presentations. During his presidential re-election campaign, he was 73 years old and got a lot of questions and criticisms about his age. He used humor to defuse that potential deficit. One of his famous quips was during a 1984 debate with his Democratic challenger, Walter Mondale. When the issue of age came up, he stated firmly that age should not be a factor in the election. "I don't think it would be fair for me to hold my opponent's youth and inexperience against him."

Sources for Humor

You might be thinking, *Gee, I'm just not a funny person. I don't know how to be humorous.* But keep in mind, incorporating humor into your talks isn't about being a comedian. It's about finding humor in everyday situations everyone can relate to. Everyone has stood in the grocery checkout line and experienced the maddening frustration of being in what feels like the slowest-moving line on the planet. Everyone has been behind the woman who waits until her $300 worth of groceries is completely rung up before she digs for her checkbook, opens it carefully to review her balance and writes out the check in a slow, careful manner, then has to dig for her ID, then puts everything slowly away. Life's frustrating moments can drive us mad while we're experiencing them. But there can be humor in telling about them because everyone can relate to those same frustrations.

So how do you find humor?

- The first place to start is your life. Take the time to find humor in your real life experiences. In my Business Etiquette workshops, participants occasionally ask about teaching children good manners. I relate this true story: "The best advice I can give is to model what you expect of them. Here's a great example. My brother

Brian and his wife Janet have a son, Clark, who's four years old. Before the holidays, I called Brian to ask if it'd be all right with him and his family if we changed our Thanksgiving celebration to Friday instead of Thursday. 'Sure, no problem,' he said. Thinking his response was a little hasty, I asked, 'Um, shouldn't you check with Janet first?' He lowered his voice and said, 'Janet and I just had a serious discussion with Clark about how you don't interrupt someone when they're talking. Well, now he and Janet are having a conversation, so… I don't dare interrupt.'" It's not a joke, but most people can relate to the challenges and surprises that children bring to our lives. The story always generates appreciative laughter.

- Use the moment. It helps during the presentation if you can be flexible and find humor on the spot. A famous speaker once got so carried away in his presentation that spit flew from his mouth. He paused and said wryly to the person closest to him, "Sorry— did I get any on you?" The audience loved it.

Perhaps you notice on your visual that a word is misspelled. Consider a quip like one speaker used: "Mark Twain once said he never respected anyone who couldn't spell a word more than one way."

Maybe, as you begin speaking into the microphone, there's loud, screeching feedback. Said one speaker, "Must be mating season for microphones."

It doesn't hurt to have some of these "ad libs" prepared. Years ago, then vice

Desserts is "stressed" backwards

Once, as an after-dinner speaker, I faced one of a speaker's greatest nightmares. I arrived at the lectern only minutes after I had just eaten a delicious ice cream dessert. I should have known better. Dairy products and cold food or drink can wreak havoc on your vocal chords.

Sure enough, as I opened my mouth to speak, nothing came out but a croak! After a few embarrassing seconds of clearing my throat, I managed to rasp, "You'll have to excuse me. Some of that delicious dessert seems to have gotten caught in my throat. If only it would stay there and not go to my thighs…"

The audience (of mostly women) roared with appreciation. And I bought myself some time to clear my throat enough to begin speaking.

president George Bush made a verbal gaffe. Instead of saying the administration had had setbacks, he said, "We've had sex." After the laughter had died down, Bush said, "I feel like the javelin thrower who won the toss and elected to receive." The story made national news and was widely regarded as being a "very good recovery." But Bush had the remark prepared in the event of just such a blunder. Try to prepare your own "ad lib" lines for the times when you need to recover from a slip-up.

- Do or say something offbeat or unexpected. I once saw a woman give a presentation on handling stress. She offered several pointers on dealing with stress, weaving humorous anecdotes throughout. One of her tips was that, regardless of how you feel on the inside, you shouldn't show it on the outside. "For example," she said, "what you see up here is a woman who's polished and put together. But you have no idea how wrecked I might be on the inside." Suddenly she flung off her suit jacket to reveal a blouse that was torn and shredded. Then she slipped her skirt off to reveal a second skirt torn and tattered, covered with safety pins and band-aids. The audience gasped at first, then broke into peals of laughter.

  My brother Steve has a great sense of humor. He recently co-chaired the "Missions" committee at his church. In order to add a little wit and creativity, he and his team called themselves the "Good News Brothers." They donned sunglasses, hats, dark suits, and ties—à la the "Blues Brothers"—complete with music, whenever they had to give a presentation to the church. The congregation loved their routine so much that they voted them "Men of the Year." At first, Steve was actually a little disappointed because he felt the award was more about them than the good works they were about. But, of course, that's the whole point. The message has much more impact if the messenger is entertaining and engaging. And humor is one of the best ways to do that.

- Another great way to incorporate humor is to use a cartoon in a visual. This can be an effective way to get a laugh without putting yourself on the line (if the audience doesn't laugh, it was the cartoon that wasn't funny to them—not you). One of my favorites I use in a presentation on public speaking is a Dilbert cartoon, where the first frame shows Dogbert saying to Dilbert, "They say that people fear public speaking more than they fear death." In the second frame he says, "So, technically, if you kill a guy who's scheduled to speak, you'd be doing him a favor."

Just a little delivery tip on using cartoons: It's better if you actually read the cartoon lines aloud to the audience. If you just let the audience read it for themselves, you'll lose a lot of impact. People read at different rates and are going to "get it" at different times. That tends to dilute the response. So read it aloud—with all the appropriate inflection.

It's in the Delivery and Timing

Once in one of my workshops, a participant presented a complicated visual with all the different aspects of the company's benefits. One of the lines referred to the allowance "per spouse." Now, that really can be a good source of humor—after all, the implication is that you might have more than one spouse. The speaker tried to play on that angle, but to his chagrin, his attempt at humor fell flat.

I gave him the following pointers on how he could have used the humor to greater effect:

First of all, on such a complicated slide, he needed to draw the audience's attention to each line as he referred to it. The more complex the visual, the more likely the audience will be reading or studying any part of it other than what you're talking about. So a funny comment about one line can be lost on the audience if they're lost in your visual. By physically pointing to the line you're discussing, you're keeping the audience's attention with you. (More on this in Chapter V—Visuals.)

Then, while pointing to the line that said "allowance per spouse," he needed to read it, emphasizing the words, *per spouse*. Then, pausing just a beat and with a wry expression, he should deliver his line: "...just in case you were worried whether all your spouses would be covered."

I once coached a woman who wanted to do comedy routines. She had great material and had mastered her unique delivery manner—a sort of deadpan, whiney style. But she neglected to recognize the importance of letting the audience laugh. No sooner did her audience start laughing at one of her lines, than she jumped right into the next line. The noise of laughter would cause the audience to miss the beginning of her next remark, which in turn, often diluted the impact of that joke. We worked on the importance of the *pause* in humor. You have to give the audience a chance to finish their laughter.

Sometimes a poignant pause can add to the humor. My mother decided in her senior years to take one of her talents—joke-telling—to the stage. She has spoken before thousands of people, delivering her perspectives on aging with a zany irreverence. Entirely self-taught in this comedy business, she has learned the value of the pause.

Lamenting the frustrations of growing older, she says, "Just when I get my head together, my body starts falling apart. But I have learned that I can smooth out the wrinkles in my face if I go braless…" This remark, so totally incongruous with the little old lady saying it, never fails to generate peals of laughter. Then, after the laughter has died down, my mother says nothing, just smiles smugly and raises one of her eyebrows. The audience roars with more laughter.

It's all in the delivery and timing.

K

Knowledge is power.
—SIR FRANCIS BACON

Knowledge

Several years ago, a client asked me, as a favor, if I'd speak before our city council on an uptown development issue. I was flattered by his request, but as I stood facing the mayor and city council members, I was suddenly petrified. First of all, I realized that I hadn't done my homework to find out exactly where the council members stood on this issue. Were my remarks singing to the choir or falling on deaf ears? I also had drafted what I thought were some good remarks—based on my limited knowledge of the issue—and delivered them as effectively as I could. But later, watching myself on the television rebroadcast of the meeting, I was humiliated. I did not appear confident or knowledgeable. I was not a powerful proponent of the issue.

What was the valuable lesson to learn here? If you don't know your audience or your subject well, you can't be a credible presenter.

Know Your Audience

This is a crucial element to the success of your presentation, yet it's amazing how often speakers neglect this basic tenet: *Know thy audience.* If you're a financial planner, you might have a great presentation to give on retirement accounts. But the talk you would give to a group of just graduated young professionals would have to be different from one to a group of people on the verge of retirement.

Knowledge

I once heard a speaker who was the author of a book about how women can get ahead in business. She was addressing a group of high-level professional women—presidents, directors, executive vice presidents, and women business owners. In other words, her audience members were already highly successful. Unfortunately, the speaker just regurgitated tidbits from her book, offering guidelines far more appropriate to the young woman just getting started in her career. She was saved by the fact that her delivery was engaging and humorous—she had some great horror stories to tell. But she could have hit a home run if she'd better tailored her remarks to her "already arrived" audience.

How do you find out who your audience is? If you're speaking to a group outside of your work, ask your contact (see Chapter G—Gigs) about the audience. What profession(s) are they in? What's the average age? What do they know about your topic? Why did they ask you to speak?

One of my volunteer activities is serving on the Speaker's Bureau for the Shelter for Battered Women where I give presentations on domestic violence (see the outline of such a speech in Chapter C—Content). I have to know the nature of the audience because my topic is a sensitive one. Men react differently than women. Older people have inbred stereotypes that younger people don't have. Ultra religious groups have different attitudes about it than more liberal ones. Knowing my audience not only helps me plan my remarks, but also prepares me for the possible questions and objections I might get.

If your audience is a group in your company, you may already know who they are and what their needs and hot buttons are (see Chapter S—Selling). But not knowing that group, especially if it's a high-level one, can be a big source of stress. Many of my workshop participants often have to deal with this. They get invited to make a presentation to a management team or other leadership group, and they're panic-stricken because they don't know what this group wants and they don't feel comfortable asking them directly. In this case, one good option is to ask associates who may work with or be familiar with those people. Administrative assistants could be a valuable source of help here. One of the key things you want to know about a high-level group is whether they are big picture- or detail-oriented. Do they prefer just the bottom line or do they want to scrutinize every step? With people much higher up the food chain than you are, it's wise to try to meet their needs.

What if you discover that your audience is a mixed bag? In this case, where you risk alienating some members while pleasing others, I'd say this would be the time to ask for direction from that group's senior person. Whether you make direct contact with a phone call or e-mail, or use an administrative assistant as the go-between, there's a good chance the executive will be flattered and impressed that you took the time to find out the best way to meet the group's needs.

If you're unable to do this, then keep this in mind. Most people who are at the upper echelons of an organization are more likely to be big picture thinkers. Their job is to plan and oversee the company's vision. They leave the detail to those in the trenches. So even if you're a detail-oriented person, the odds are you'll be more successful in a presentation to upper management if you trim all the step-by-step methods and focus on the end result. Make sure you have a handout or backup visual that covers the details should anyone ask.

Know Your Subject

It's as simple as this: Never speak on a topic you don't know well. Your confidence level isn't going to be as high, which will undoubtedly increase your nervousness and discomfort. Your delivery may suffer as you try to appear more confident than you feel. And you just might get nailed during the Q&A session when you try to answer questions on a subject you're not that familiar with.

As I learned from my city council presentation, just because you might be a "good" speaker doesn't mean you can handle any topic. As you develop your knowledge and skill in an area, making presentations on that subject can be a great way to expose others to your expertise. But until you have that comfortable level of proficiency on a subject, you'll find that trying to present on it can undermine your credibility and power.

L

Likability

When I conduct a Presentation Skills seminar, I ask every participant to complete a questionnaire prior to attending. One of the questions is, "What do you believe are your strengths or assets as a public speaker?" Following that is the question, "What are your challenges or weaknesses?" The vast majority of respondents are fairly humble in recounting their strengths and pretty hard on themselves when reciting their weaknesses.

But every once in a while, I get a questionnaire back where the respondent is downright glowing in naming strengths (*I'm very comfortable speaking. I have lots of experience. My delivery is dynamic. I'm well organized. I'm good with humor.*) and can't seem to acknowledge any weaknesses (*I'm taking this because my manager signed me up.*). Inevitably in the workshop, I discover an interesting anomaly about those speakers. Yes, their technical skills are indeed good. But something's off. It usually boils down to the fact that they're often simply not *likable*.

This is a very subjective area. I may like someone you don't, or vice versa, for all kinds of reasons. Still, there are some universal qualities that make up likability. If you want to influence the audience—persuade them or move them—then there's no question you will be more successful if the audience feels warmly and positively about you. If you come across as arrogant, uncaring, or cold, an audience is much less likely to be influenced by your message.

Traits of Likability

An effective speaker will not only have a dynamic delivery and well-organized and humanizing content, but will also be likable. Here are a few qualities that influence likability:

- **Audience-focused.** A speaker who's self-centered, concerned mostly about appearances and the technicalities of the presentation, is going to have a hard time connecting with the audience. I mentioned in Chapter A—Anxiety that focusing on the audience—instead of yourself—can help bring down your anxiety level. The bonus is that if you genuinely care about your audience, the listeners will feel much more receptive to you.

- **Confident but humble.** You're knowledgeable about your field, earned your stripes, and paid your dues. Aren't you entitled to a healthy dose of ego? Won't audiences question your credibility if you're not confident and sure of yourself? Confidence is an attractive trait. But arrogance is not. What's the difference? Arrogance is me-focused: *Look at me. Look what I've accomplished. Look what I can do.* Confidence is other-focused: *This is a great team. I couldn't have done it without her. I'm so proud of you.* As a speaker, you want to appear confident, but not arrogant. It's the difference between extolling the virtues of a project versus taking all the credit for its creation.

  One typical example of how arrogance can be manifested is the way someone gets started. Undoubtedly you've experienced the speaker who comes on stage, says, "Good morning," and gets a handful of mumbles back. He pauses, then says louder, "I *said*, GOOD MORNING!" And of course, the audience feels compelled to yell "Good morning!" back. What purpose does this accomplish? Such a speaker might argue that it creates energy and excitement in the audience. But a good speaker will naturally generate that enthusiasm in his presentation. Forcing the audience to be loud and responsive right out of the gate is more about stroking the speaker's ego than building liveliness in the crowd. Be confident about your subject, but humble about yourself.

- **Good listener.** This may seem a little ironic. How can the speaker also be a good listener? Most presentations involve some kind of interaction with the audience, whether it's a Q&A session, a discussion of the issues you've presented, or a facilitation of the meeting. Your ability to give others the floor, listen actively to them (see Chapter O—Other Communication), and give appropriate, thoughtful responses to their input will make you more likable.

- **Interest in others.** The ability to show interest, concern, and a sort of wide-eyed wonder in what others have to say is the kind of skill that will make people think positively and warmly about you. Especially when you're in the "power seat" of being the presenter, it's a compelling trait to give up the floor to others because you're genuinely interested in what they have to say.

- **Humor.** Everyone likes to laugh. Laughter makes us feel good. If you have the ability to make your audience laugh, there's no question they'll like you more. Remember the warning in the previous chapter about telling jokes. A joke that's offensive or a real moaner is not going to win over your audience. Humor that comes from your everyday life can be more effective than canned jokes. The more you can show the audience you're comfortable poking fun at yourself, the more you'll endear yourself to them.

- **Pleasant attitude.** People who are pessimistic, negative, and complaining are magnets only for the same type of people. Most of us prefer people who are positive and upbeat, who seem to be enjoying life and having a good time. Like the song says, be happy. Smile.

- **Empathy.** This trait is useful in the Q&A session when you might get questioners who are upset and confused (see Chapter R—Rising Above…). Remember that this presentation is not just about you. Empathize with people's confusion over the issue or frustration with the new changes. It'll make you one of them and therefore more likable.

- **Not preachy.** Your goal as a speaker is to inform or persuade, not to lecture or sermonize. You want to be careful that your tone is not admonishing your audience. One example of this type of attitude is when a speaker calls on audience members out of the blue. *Jim, what do you think of that?* Poor Jim's attention might have been wandering right then, or perhaps he doesn't know what he thinks about it or doesn't want to share it. He has been put on the spot by the speaker and will have a difficult time wriggling his way out of it. That's not going to endear him to the speaker.

- **Purposeful.** There's that word again—purposeful. Creative humanizing elements can make a presentation more interesting and meaningful, but like everything else about your presentation, they need to have some kind of purpose. If a speaker tells stories (or jokes) that don't seem to relate to the topic, if she pulls little gimmicks for the sake of being cute but they have no relevance to the issue, audiences can get confused or frustrated.

For example, one such non-purposeful technique is the speaker who simply calls audience members by name for no obvious reason: *Joe, we've had such a great year. Let's take advantage of it, Cindy. Fred, I've got just the solution.* I've seen speakers do this in the interest of audience involvement. But it's not really involving them. Remember in grade school when the teacher would say a student's name in the middle of her instruction? She did it because she could tell the student wasn't paying attention. It was a verbal rap on the knuckles to get the child's attention. That kind of behavior for an adult may evoke that same feeling of a slight reprimand— not something that will make you likable to the audience.

I'm not suggesting that you should never call audience members by name. In answering someone's question or directing a comment specifically to one person, using the individual's name can be a nice personal touch. It's only when it's not purposeful that it sounds gratuitous.

M

Microphone

If you've ever been in an audience where you had difficulty hearing or understanding a speaker, you know the frustration that occurs when a speaker doesn't use a microphone properly.

For talking to a large group, using a microphone is a given for a speaker. I'm going to share a few tips to help you use one effectively. But here's my overriding advice: *Always ask for a lavaliere mike.* A lavaliere (or lapel mike) is a battery-operated microphone that clips to your lapel or collar and has a wire that runs to the pocket-sized transmitter, which you attach to your waistband. This system allows you freedom of movement; you don't have to be tied to a lectern or inconvenienced by holding a handheld mike.

I've heard speakers complain that the facility where they were speaking didn't provide a lavaliere, so they were stuck with the mike on the lectern. But here's the thing—ask for it. I always ask for a lavaliere for my speaking engagements and it's extremely rare that my request has ever been refused. Almost all facilities have these mikes available—or can rent them—so you're not making an unusual request.

A Few Tips on Lavalieres

If you want to have an engaging presence and be able to project your full dynamism, you need the freedom of movement that a lavaliere provides.

- Try to wear the clip-on transmitter in an unobtrusive location. Clipped to your waistband against your back is the best place. Ideally, you can wear a jacket or untucked sweater or top that will hide it. Before fastening the mike onto your lapel, run the wire up underneath your jacket or shirt so it's not visible and won't get in your way when you make all those great gestures.

- Dress accordingly. This usually isn't a problem for men, whose wardrobe choices always include a waistband for attaching the transmitter and some kind of jacket lapel or shirt collar onto which to fasten the mike. But women have more clothing options, some of which aren't conducive to wearing a lavaliere. A dress with no waistline means no place to secure the transmitter. A top without a stand-up collar or lapel will require the microphone to be fastened on the neck opening. This may cause the mike to rub against the neck or collarbone, which not only might be uncomfortable but could also create some sound problems. So give particular thought to what you're going to wear when you'll be speaking with a lavaliere.

- Always perform a sound check before your presentation. This will give you an idea of how you're projecting and if you need to clip the mike closer to or farther away from your face.

- Make sure you know how to turn the transmitter on and off. If you're wearing it before and after your talk, you don't want it on where it will catch any of your off-stage conversations, or heaven forbid, your trip to the restroom.

Tips on Handheld Microphones

If a lavaliere mike isn't available, then a handheld one is the next best choice. Although you will have to hold it, you still have that freedom of movement so important to your dynamism.

- Request a cordless mike. That way, you don't have to worry about the cord. A cord can be distracting—I've seen speakers play with it as if it were a lasso. It can also be dangerous, increasing the risk you might trip over it. A cordless mike is safer and less distracting to use. Its main disadvantage is that it's battery-operated, so you need to be sensitive to not running the battery down.

- Hold it roughly two to four inches from your mouth.
- Conduct a sound check ahead of time so that you know exactly how you need to hold the mike to get the best projection. Talking too close may create too much amplification, but holding it too far away may not pick up your voice adequately.
- If the mike is cordless, know how to turn it on and off so it doesn't pick up extraneous conversation (and doesn't wear the battery down).
- Always make sure the mike follows your head movements. If you turn your head to the side, move the microphone, too, so that it's always in front of your mouth.

Tips on Lectern Microphones

First of all, let's clear up some vernacular. A **lectern** is the correct name to refer to the stand that a speaker uses for notes and on which a microphone is placed. The term **podium** is often used interchangeably with this word, and while not a big deal, it's helpful to know that technically, the podium is actually the raised dais or platform that a speaker might stand on.

- Adjust the angle of the mike and your own position so your mouth is roughly two to four inches from the mike.
- Do a sound check ahead of time. Mikes are different quality—some will be able to pick up your voice even if you're several inches away and have turned your face to the side. Others pick up little unless your mouth is practically right on top of it. The safest thing is to act as if the mike doesn't have great range. So this means speaking directly into it. Be careful if you drop your chin to look at notes or turn your head to refer to a visual that it doesn't cause the audience to lose your voice.
- You want, of course, to make good eye contact around the room. But don't turn your head from side to side. This will mean that your mouth will not always be directly in line with the mike. Instead, learn to angle your whole body subtly from side to side so that at all times the microphone is lined up with your mouth.
- Keep in mind that a lectern, while handy for holding your notes, has the drawback of placing a barrier between you and your audience. It's even more important to project energy when you're trapped behind a lectern.

N

Experience is the name everyone gives to their mistakes.

—OSCAR WILDE

No-Nos

Any number of things can diminish your power and effectiveness as a speaker. While they've been covered in the relevant chapters in this book, I thought I'd list them here as a quick reference.

Presentation No-Nos:

- Don't read from your notes. This will give you a flat, canned delivery. Talk to your audience; don't read to them.
- Don't read from your visual. This puts more of your attention on the screen than on the audience. Refer to the visual, but talk to the audience.
- Don't regurgitate a long list of facts, figures, or statistics. If all you do is recite the data, then there's no need for you to be there. The audience can read the report. Your job as a speaker is to *humanize* the information, to give it meaning and interest.
- Avoid not looking at the audience. Poor eye communication prevents a connection with your audience. At best, it makes you look uncomfortable—at worst, dishonest. Look at and talk to audience members individually.
- Avoid using overly busy visual aids. If the audience has to spend all its time trying to decipher your visuals, there's not going to be any focus on you.

- Don't have too many visuals. If you're basically presenting a slide show, why are you there? Use visuals to complement your presentation, not *be* it.
- Don't appear arrogant and self-centered. You can't connect with an audience if you care only about yourself. Be confident about your topic but humble about yourself.
- Don't ramble. Get to the point. Audiences don't want to struggle to understand you and will eventually tune you out if they can't follow you. Organize your thoughts and follow a clear outline.
- Don't exceed the time limit you've been allotted. This shows a lack of respect for your audience's time, as well as for any other speakers on the agenda. Know your time limit and prepare your remarks so that you'll finish within the time limit.
- Don't fail to relate to your audience. If you talk above—or below—your audience's head, you'll only manage to antagonize them. Know your audience and relate to their interest in and knowledge of the subject.
- Avoid dodging questions. If you evade a question or answer dishonestly, the audience will doubt your credibility on the whole subject. If you don't know an answer, or can't answer a sensitive question, be honest.
- Avoid not listening to a questioner. Don't be so eager to answer the question that you don't give the questioner time to ask. Questioners want to be heard. Force yourself to pause before you answer every question.
- Don't lose your cool with a difficult or tough audience member. Getting defensive or angry will make you a villain in the audience's eyes. If you keep your cool and stay focused on the issue when someone is giving you a hard time, audience members will be more likely to see you as a victim and be sympathetic.
- Don't hog the limelight when you're introducing another speaker. Your objective is to make the speaker look good. Make your introduction complete but brief.
- Don't ignore the microphone. If the audience can't pick up what you're saying or has to strain to hear you, you're not creating a situation conducive to getting your message across. Always speak

into the microphone, with your mouth two to four inches away from it.

- Don't use off-color or inappropriate humor. Unless you really, really know your audience well, it's a huge gamble to use a little risqué humor. Finding humor from your everyday life is safer, and often funnier, than a dirty joke.

- Don't panic at the slightest misstep. If you have a case of the "gotta be perfects," you're not going to be able to give a relaxed, comfortable presentation. Lighten up. Audiences will be very forgiving of those occasional little glitches. Learn to say, "So what?" when things don't go perfectly.

- Don't hold your arms in any closed or tight resting place. Standing in a fig leaf or arm clutch, or with hands on hips, crossed arms, or hands in pockets, will not convey confidence and poise. Instead think of open and fluid—parade rest, arms at the side, one arm up, both arms up.

- Avoid too many "ums" or other nonword fillers. They make you sound tentative and unsure and are extremely distracting if overdone. Learn to pause instead.

- Don't speak in a deadly dull monotone. Nothing will tune an audience out faster. Put energy and interest in your voice. Employ vocal variety.

- Avoid pacing, "dancing," or other non-purposeful movement. This serves only to make you look nervous or uncomfortable. Remember that any movement that's purposeful has power.

- Avoid a low-key, ho-hum delivery. If you can't get excited about your topic, your audience sure can't. Showing conviction and passion through a dynamic delivery will make you more engaging and have the audience hanging on your every word.

O

Other Communication

> *I wish people who have trouble communicating would just shut up.*
> —TOM LEHRER

Many times in my workshops, participants complain that they don't really give all that many formal presentations. They claim they'd be better served if they could learn how to run a meeting or make a sales call or have better communication with the boss or a colleague. Well, guess what? Almost every skill that can make you a more compelling presenter is going to enhance all those other communication situations. In fact, among all the guidelines for standing out when you stand up, there is only *one difference* between a formal, stand-up presentation and a more informal, seated meeting or interaction. Everything else is the same.

Good Communication Qualities

Before we address that one difference, let's review those qualities that are going to serve you well regardless of the communication situation:

- Know your audience.
- Convey enthusiasm and energy for what you're talking about.
- Be pleasant. Smile.
- Make eye communication with your audience/listener.
- Avoid nervous, distracting mannerisms.

- Remember that your clothing communicates.
- Use purposeful gestures.
- Put expression in your vocals.
- Minimize the "ums."
- Humanize your content to make it interesting and memorable.
- Be prepared for questions and know how to handle tough questions and tough questioners.
- If you have visuals in the form of handouts, make them simple and readable.
- Organize your thoughts in the outline form:
    - –Set it up—a road map or agenda
    - –Tell what's up—the main points or basic concept
    - –Wrap it up—summarize, next steps, ask for the sale
- If your purpose is persuasive, organize your thoughts according to whether your objective is to get your listener to do something (Action), believe something is true (Fact), or be persuaded that one solution is better than another (Value).
- Be sure to use motivational appeals when you want to persuade.
- Honor the time limit you've been given.

The One Difference

Obviously, the primary difference between a standing presentation and a seated conversation is your *posture*. And it's the guideline for that posture that has a different rule for seated than for standing:

- When *standing*, a balanced, *symmetrical* posture is more poised and confident.
- When *seated*, an *asymmetrical*, off-balance posture is more poised and confident: Think in terms of crossed legs and arms not mirroring each other, such as, one arm propped at chin and the other on the table, or one arm resting on arm of chair with the other hand in your lap.

This is an interesting thing to observe. Picture a speaker standing with one leg crossed in front of the other, leaning all his weight on one leg, and one hand clasping the other arm. This asymmetrical posture doesn't conjure up a look of confidence or ease, does it?

When your weight is evenly distributed on both feet and your resting places have a fairly symmetrical look about them, you look more poised.

But apply those qualities to someone who's seated. Can you envision someone sitting with both feet on the floor, and hands resting symmetrically in the lap or on the arms of the chair? That doesn't look very comfortable, does it?

Instead, envision her with her legs crossed, with one arm up and one arm down.

Can you see how this asymmetrical posture is a more poised and comfortable look?

Think of people sitting around a table. Can you see the difference between someone whose arms are positioned symmetrically—perhaps hands clasped or arms folded or fingertips steepled—and someone whose arms are asymmetrical, such as one hand up at chin with the other down, or one hand holding a pen? When you're standing, a balanced, symmetrical pose looks more confident. But when you're seated, an unbalanced, asymmetrical pose looks more at ease.

There are a few other guidelines that can help your communication in the more informal, seated meeting or conversation.

- Show interest in others.
- Ask them questions.
- Don't monopolize the conversation.
- Remember personal details about them.
- Mirror the other person's style.
- Be a good listener.

Listening

I'm including listening in this chapter because it's not only an excellent skill for a speaker to possess, but it's one of the most powerful communication skills there is. Good listening has the ability to defuse conflict, enhance understanding, and put you in control of the situation. Being an effective listener is not just a skill you can develop, but a gift you give others because it fulfills two basic human needs: to be heard and to be understood.

There is a right way to listen, called *active listening*. It involves three steps, which I remember by using the acronym EAR:

Engage the speaker. Show the speaker you're listening by looking him in the eye, nodding occasionally, showing appropriate facial expressions (a smile for good news, concern for distressing news). Project open and relaxed body language. Also keep in mind that total silence does not imply listening. Give vocal signals such as: *mm-hmm, yes, really?, I see,* and so forth.

Actually hear. This means you have to pay attention and hear what's actually being said. You must concentrate on the *content* of the message, which is what the speaker is saying, plus the *intent*, which is what she's feeling or what she means. It helps to force yourself to follow along if you repeat her key words or main ideas to yourself and also observe the nonverbal cues she's giving. Taking notes is an effective way to follow the speaker's thoughts. If you don't agree with the speaker, it's a particularly effective exercise to try to put yourself in her shoes and see it from her perspective.

Respond appropriately. This third step is the key to effectively wielding the power of listening. Instead of the standard "Yes, but…" response we're all so conditioned to reply with, this step lets the other person feel that you heard and understood him. It can pay powerful dividends in human relations. Appropriate responses can occur three ways:

- **Paraphrase**. Repeat the gist of the message. It is generally preceded by, *So what you're saying is…* or *In other words…* or *If I understand you correctly….* This lets the speaker know you did, in fact, hear the content of what he said. It's important to understand that paraphrasing does not mean agreement. Saying, *In other words, you feel that the level of work you've done this year is worth a $10,000 increase in salary,* does not mean you agree with it. The amazing thing about paraphrasing is that once people feel like you heard them, they are more receptive and open to what you have to say.

- **Probe**. This is particularly effective when you disagree with the speaker. When we disagree with someone, it's so tempting to reply, *Yes, but…* or *I understand, but….* This generally creates a vicious cycle of butting heads. Instead of rebutting immediately, ask questions of the speaker to gain more information and understanding. *Why do you say that? How do you think that will work? How did you come to that conclusion?* If a speaker is given more opportunity to elaborate, either you will come to gain more understanding or she might talk herself out of her position.

- **Reflect** back feelings. Reflecting is the more finely tuned skill of interpreting how the speaker feels about what he said. *You must be so proud,* or *That certainly must have made you angry,* or *I imagine you're very hurt by that…* are examples of reflecting. This is the ultimate validation a speaker can receive: being heard and being understood. When you give that gift to others, it opens doors, breaks down barriers, diffuses anger, and decreases resistance.

P

In the United States all business not transacted over the telephone is accomplished in conjunction with alcohol or food, often under conditions of advanced intoxication.

—JOHN KENNETH GALBRAITH

Phone Conference

Face-to-face meetings are becoming increasingly rare today. Many business meetings are now often conducted via teleconference. Dozens or scores of people from all across the country, or even the world, "meet" and make presentations in a conference call.

The Challenges of Teleconferencing

Making a presentation in this venue presents many unique challenges. First of all, remember from the Mehrabian statistics that our nonverbals are the largest part of our communication impact? Consider what that does to our impact when we take that element away.

Then there's the dilemma of whether to mute or not to mute. When the conference participants put their phones on mute, it omits any distracting background noise. But the speaker faces the unnerving situation of talking to dead air, which feels disturbingly as if no one is listening. If phones are not muted, then there's the annoyance of background noise—ringing phones, voices, feedback from speaker phones, the clacking of keys on a keyboard.

In either case, muted or not, there are still some people who simply aren't paying attention. They're reading and sending e-mails or working on some other task, giving only half an ear to the proceedings. There's also the difficulty of having someone interject a comment or ask a question, and the speaker has no idea who's spoken.

It's a challenging and intimidating situation. While this venue is fraught with pitfalls and distractions, I can offer a few tips for making as effective a teleconference presentation as possible.

Guidelines for Effective Phone Conferences

Most of the rules of presentations apply:

- Have your content well organized. Make an outline of your presentation and include a good road map so everyone knows where you're headed. Announce at the beginning of your presentation whether you would prefer listeners hold all questions until the end, or if they can make inquiries as you go along.
- Recognize that now that your nonverbals no longer play a part, your vocal qualities are crucial. Make sure there is energy in your voice, that you vary your rate and volume and use inflection. Smile while you talk. A monotone voice over the phone is a sure way to tune out your listeners.
- The keep-it-simple rule still applies to visuals. Many teleconferences are conducted with an accompanying computer slide show or web-conferencing site so that the listeners can follow along on their computer screens while the speaker is presenting. If your visuals are wordy and complex, your audience is going to be reading them instead of listening to you. They can easily get ahead of you (people read faster than you can talk) and you'll lose them. Strive to make your visuals complement and reinforce what you're saying, not stand alone.

In addition, there are a few other guidelines that can help with the unique challenge of presenting in a phone conference:

- Learn how to use the teleconferencing system. Various telephone conference vendors offer different features. Find out if there is a "moderator's line" that allows you to mute out all other callers during the main body of your presentation. Then, find out how to reopen the lines for Q&A. Before beginning your presentation, remind all attendees to use appropriate phone etiquette. Ask them to mute their lines, if necessary, and to avoid calling in on cell phones or speaker phones since they can cause static and feedback.

- One good technique to try to ensure active listening from the group is to make a point of inviting participants' contributions. You could even cue them ahead of time: *Jane, just so you know, during my presentation in tomorrow's conference call, I'm going to ask you to give an update on your department's progress on the Six Sigma project.* If you do that with several people, they'll know they're going to be called on and will be more likely to be attentive during your presentation. Others who are listening may become aware that you're soliciting comments from others and may be more motivated to pay attention in case you call on them.

- Finally, I'd like to ask you a question. When you're a listener on a phone conference, do you model the behavior you'd like listeners to exhibit when you're speaking? If we all practiced good teleconference etiquette—paying attention, staying away from e-mail and other tasks, asking questions or making comments when appropriate—the phone conference would be a much less frustrating exchange.

This is as good a place as any in this book to mention audience etiquette in general. Speakers and audiences have an unspoken contract. The speaker agrees to provide valuable information that will inform or persuade the audience and to honor the time limit allotted. The audience agrees to listen respectfully, ask questions if necessary, and not derail or upstage the speaker. If you want an audience to uphold their end of the bargain when you're the speaker, then remember to honor that contract when you're a member of the audience.

Q

Q&A

"Are there any questions?" With those words, you kick off a deceptively important part of your presentation. Because the Q&A session is perceived as being "off the cuff," the audience instinctively believes they're going to find out what you really know. So you don't want to risk blowing it—stumbling over a question, getting defensive, looking stupid. Handling questions with composure is a crucial part of your presentation. This is often where you win or lose the audience's respect.

So you need to prepare for the Q&A. "What?" you ask. "How can I possibly prepare for Q&A? I can't predict what questions I'm going to be asked!" Ah, therein lies the potential downfall of the most polished speaker—not being prepared for the questions that may be asked.

I'm going to use a Q&A format to share some basic guidelines for handling questions and remaining unflappable under pressure. But before I do, let me just give one caveat: Don't give a talk on a subject you don't know well. You may be able to put together a great presentation, but you'll get nailed in the Q&A. So know your subject. Also know your audience. Their familiarity with or attitude toward your topic can give you an idea of the kinds of questions you might receive.

Q&A

What Will the Audience Ask You?

Anticipate what you'll be asked so you'll be prepared with good answers. Ideally, invite a group of colleagues to come up with questions—especially tough ones—so you can practice the answers. Get feedback from other people familiar with the topic so you can agree on how to address sensitive issues.

What If They Don't Ask You Any Questions?

When no one asks any questions, it'd be nice to think, *Gee, I must have done such a good job of covering the subject that no one needs to ask anything additional.* But unfortunately, the feeling is more of a letdown. *Gosh, no one's interested. I must not have done a good job.* In actuality, of course, the real reason no one responds to your request for questions is probably somewhere in between. Often no one likes to be the first to speak up. Some people might be afraid of asking a dumb question. It may be that the Q&A simply needs a kick-start. So if you don't get any questions at first, consider the following techniques.

- Try introducing one yourself: *A question I'm often asked is....* This is easier to do, of course, if you've anticipated some questions. Your starting off with a question and then discussing the answer could be a springboard to other audience questions.
- Another tactic is to refer to a conversation you might have had earlier with an audience member. Often when you mingle with the audience before your talk or during a break, they will inevitably ask you something about your topic. So this might be a good place to refer to that (as long as it's not embarrassing to the questioner): *On the break, Sam asked me about....*
- You could also try asking some of your own: *Well, let me ask you. How many of you have had problems with this new program?* This might lead to other questions or just to a lively discussion that involves some audience participation.

What If You Don't Know an Answer to a Question?

Please, please, if you don't know an answer, be honest. Either ask your audience for help *(Does anyone here know how that process works?)*

or promise to find out and get back to the questioner. Admittedly, it can be tough to say *I don't know*, especially if you should know the answer. Here's a face-saving method to avoid that. Instead say: *That's a good question—I've never gotten that before. Let me research it and get back to you.*

How Do I Structure the Answer to a Question?

Although Q&A is a great opportunity to showcase your grasp of the issue, a good speaker recognizes that every answer is not another speech. You want your answer to be brief—yet complete—so you can field as many questions as possible. Here's a good format to use that will help you express concise, appropriate answers. I call it the **ABC** formula:

Answer the question as directly as possible. If you immediately launch into background or try to sidestep, the audience may question your motives.

Background. Give reasons, examples, and explanations about your answer, if necessary.

Connect to the key idea or main theme you want to get across. In many presentations, there's a key message the speaker wants to underscore. It might be that the project is under budget, or the speaker's company has the most directly related experience for the job, or that our children are the future. Whatever it is, the Q&A is a perfect opportunity to reinforce that key message again and again by connecting answers to it.

For example, in a presentation on weight lifting for women, the speaker's main theme was that strength training is beneficial for women because it can prevent osteoporosis. Question (from a woman): "Won't lifting weights make me look muscle-bound and masculine?"

Answer: *No it won't. In fact, it will make you look more trim and toned.*

Background: *You could bulk up if you used super heavy weights and took steroids. But a simple 30-minute workout with moderate weights can help you lose weight and trim inches.*

Connect: *And don't forget, one of women's greatest health risks when* *they age is osteoporosis, resulting in poor posture and fractures. Weight training just twice a week can prevent that from happening.*

A couple other things to consider when answering a question:

- **Repeating the question.** If you're addressing a large audience where you're using a microphone, be sure to repeat an audience member's question before you answer it as a courtesy to those who couldn't hear the inquirer. This is not necessary in a small group, only in a large one where a questioner's voice won't carry without a mike. Another option for situations where you expect questions from a large audience is to arrange for microphones to be set up in the aisles for questions from the floor.

- **"Good question."** I often hear speakers compliment questions: *That's a good question.* While there's nothing wrong with this per se, the problem occurs when you overdo it. If you compliment virtually every question, it starts to look a little insincere and more like you're buying some time before you answer the question. There's also the possibility that you may be perceived as grading the questions—if you say hers was good, but not mine, are you implying my question was bad? While I may compliment a question once in a while, my usual way of handling a "good" question is to express appreciation. *I'm so glad you asked that* or *Thank you for bringing up an important issue.*

How Do You Handle Tough Questions—or Posers?

These are the really difficult questions, the ones you'd rather not answer. The first thing to remember is **buy time to think**. Here are the ways to do this:

- Repeat or paraphrase the question.
- Ask the questioner to clarify the question.
- Ask for the time: "Hmm, let me think about that a minute."
- Pause. This is a powerful technique and most effective if you use it *consistently* before you answer, whether the question is difficult or not. That way you're not broadcasting when a particular one has stumped you.

Here are some techniques for different categories of posers:

- **Complex or confusing.** Ask to have the question repeated or clarified or defined. Often, given a chance, the questioner will clear up the confusion and point you in the right direction for an answer.

- **Inappropriate.** For the NOYB variety (none of your business), simply be honest. *I'm sorry, but that's client privileged information.*

- **Framed with misleading information.** If a questioner frames a question with misleading or false information, you must correct the misleading information before you answer the question. Once a participant in one of my Business and Social Dynamics workshops asked, "Now that AIDS is such a threat in today's world, do you think the handshake will go out of style?" This was a classic case of framing the question with misleading information—that you can catch AIDS with a handshake. So the first thing I said was, "It has been unequivocally established that you cannot contract AIDS by any kind of casual touch. The common cold, maybe. But not AIDS." Then I answered the question, "So, no, the handshake is in no danger of becoming extinct. It is simply a form of greeting that will always mark us as being warm and professional."

- **Intimidating.** These kinds of questions are designed to make you squirm, because they're related to sensitive issues. They can be a bit challenging. If a direct, truthful answer may open a bigger can of worms, a little professional hedging may be in order.

Q: *Are there going to be more layoffs?*

You may choose to *discuss* the issue:

A: *It's understandable that you're concerned with layoffs. But what should be of greater concern is how we're going to pull together as a team to help this company reach its goals. The more successful we are at that, the more secure our jobs will be.*

Or you may decide to tactfully *not answer* the question:

A: *I don't believe there's any way to confirm that right now.*

Resist ever saying "no comment." That's an automatic red flag to your audience. They will understandably believe you have something to hide, so your credibility on all the other issues will suffer.

- **No win.** Some questions are framed for a yes or no response, but in a way that either answer gets you in trouble. In the speaking world, this type of query is often referred to as the "Are you still beating your wife?" question. Even by saying no, you could be implying that you used to... There's a great Dilbert cartoon where Catbert asks Dilbert, "Would you work harder if we offered stock incentives?" When Dilbert says yes, Catbert immediately responds, "So you admit you're not working hard enough now?" That's the problem with these "no-win" questions. So you can't fall into the trap of answering the question directly. Instead, you have to reframe your response.

  Q: *Have you told more lies to advance your career?*

  A: Not, *No, of course not.* (implying not *more* lies, just the old ones I've told before...)

  Instead, *I have always told the truth.*

- **Negative language or insinuations.** If a questioner uses any kind of negative language in a question, it can be disastrous to repeat the offending wordage, even if it's a denial. A classic example is the late President Nixon when he was interviewed about Watergate. In response to the accusation, he declared, "I am not a crook." Of course, that one sentence made headlines and became the catchphrase for Nixon, dogging him the rest of his days. It'd be interesting to know what would have happened if he'd simply said, "I have always strived to be honest and fair and hard-working...." Wouldn't have made quite the same sound bite, would it?

  Q: *Why are your executives paid such exorbitant salaries?*

  A: Not, *Our executives are not paid exorbitant salaries.*

  Instead, *Our executives are compensated in line with industry standards.*

These have been guidelines for dealing with tough questions. Tough *questioners* are another challenge for speakers. That's covered in Chapter R—Rising Above... (difficult audience members).

How Do You End a Q&A Session?

You exhibit more power and professionalism if you end your Q&A session with a good closing statement. Without that closing, what are your options? Generally, one of two things happens. After an uncomfortably long pause when you realize there aren't going to be any questions, you hem and haw trying to find some way to end: *Um, okay, if there aren't any more questions, well then, okay, thanks.* Or, someone else—a moderator or meeting leader—unceremoniously takes the end away from you: *Okay, thank you, Mr. Jones. And now our next speaker...."*

If, on the other hand, you can close your Q&A in a meaningful and memorable way, you have created a professional and gracious end to your whole talk. So consider this technique: Insert the Q&A session between your summary and your conclusion. Open the floor for questions *after* you've done your summary, but *before* you deliver your close.

Say you'd been giving a talk about fire safety and prevention in the home. You would wrap up your remarks with any final takeaways you wanted the audience to get, perhaps a reminder to have an escape plan for their home or to replace their smoke batteries every year. Then you could say, *Now, before I close, are there any questions?* This way you've cued the audience that you're not done. You can field the questions and when you're out of time or there seem to be no more questions, you would deliver your closing statement: *In closing, I'd just like to thank you for allowing me to share my thoughts on this important issue. Please remember, to paraphrase Smokey the Bear, only you can prevent house fires.*

What Do You Do When You're Running Out of Time?

If you're running out of time during the Q&A, resist the temptation to say, *I'll take one last question.* You could trap yourself into ending your Q&A on a really tough, negative, or antagonistic question.

I remember being on a program years ago at a company meeting. The CEO was also a speaker, and after a brief presentation, he took questions. Finally, he looked at his watch and said, "Okay, I've got time for one more question." Suddenly, a man sitting near the front, directly in front of the CEO, stood up waving his hand wildly. The CEO looked desperately around the room. When no other hands went up, he quipped, "Well, from anyone except Fred, that is…" It got a laugh. Clearly the CEO and other employees knew something about "Fred" and his issue. The CEO obviously didn't want to end his talk fielding Fred's comments. Quickly an assistant stepped up and literally whisked the CEO off the stage (and to his waiting helicopter). This was undoubtedly not the best way for this executive to end his session with his employees.

It's not wise to signal that you're taking the last question. You might be trapped into ending your session on some tough, harrowing question. You might also subtly offend those audience members who don't get selected for that last question. The best thing to do is keep it open: *Are there any more questions?* That way you can control when you want to end it. After you've answered the last question you're going to, you then simply move to your closing statement.

How Do You Remain Unflappable Under Pressure?

Finally, because Q&A may put you on the hot seat, you want to appear unflappable under pressure.

- First of all, remember that your delivery skills are just as important here as they were during your presentation. Be mindful of your balanced stance, good eye communication, and avoiding distracting mannerisms. Remember that "parade rest" is a great listening pose during Q&A—but that you need to come out of it when you start talking.

- Be particularly aware of what your body language could be signaling. For example, while a questioner is speaking, reciting a long list of all your perceived wrongs, you might naturally nod occasionally as a show of listening. But recognize how that might look nonverbally—it's as if you were agreeing with the questioner! Also be careful of other nonverbal tendencies, such as grimacing or shaking your head in response to unpleasant questions. You might not be aware of it, but the audience can sure see it. I've seen some speakers who, in reaction to a particularly tough question, backed away from the questioner as they responded. Think of the nonverbal message that sends.

- Share eye communication with all audience members. It's natural to want to talk to the person who has asked the question. But be aware you're still addressing a group. You don't want to be perceived as having a conversation with just one person. Try to start your answer by addressing the questioner, then transition to the whole audience as you get into your answer, and finally conclude by looking again at the questioner. This can cue you as to whether you've answered the question adequately—a confused or puzzled look will let you know you haven't. It also gives the questioner an opportunity for a follow-up. But you've avoided talking to just that one person.

- Avoid saying, *Did that answer your question?* When you do this, particularly if you make a habit of it, you're sending a signal that *you* don't think you answered the question. This is not going to enhance your image of confidence. If you're not sure of what the questioner is asking, get it clarified before you answer, not after.

- Listen well. This may be one of the hardest skills to practice as a speaker. After all, you're there to *speak*, right? But questioners want to be heard. So don't interrupt them and listen carefully to what they're asking. Even if you're convinced you know where the question is going, let the questioner complete his or her thoughts. The best technique to ensure this is to practice a *consistent pause* before you answer every question. If you force yourself to allow a beat or two after the questioner has spoken before you reply, then you minimize the chances that you might actually start talking before the questioner is finished. The pause is a very effective technique. Another reason it's so powerful is explained in the last point.

- Take time to think. Imagine a speaker confidently fielding questions. After each of several questions, she replies immediately and confidently. Suddenly, a questioner asks something unexpected or sensitive. What's her likely impulse? A pause. With that one pause, she has just telegraphed to the audience that she's stumped. The audience knows that one question got her, so they may wonder how valid her answer will be. The best way to avoid this characterization is to pause every time before every answer. If you do it consistently, then the message you're sending is that you're giving careful thought to every question. This is not an easy thing to do. So you're going to have to be very deliberate and intentional about it. But you'd be amazed at the difference in your presence if you pause consistently.

R

> *The problem is not that there are problems. The problem is expecting otherwise and thinking that having problems is a problem.*
>
> —THEODORE RUBIN

Rising Above...

Let's face it. People can be one of the most common sources of problems for speakers. Interrupters, bullies, show-stealers, and other problem participants challenge a speaker to rise above the adversity caused by difficult people.

Clients often ask me how to handle an audience member who's antagonistic or rude, who's nonresponsive, who has his own agenda, who contradicts you at every turn. What my participants really want to know, of course, is how they can "fix" those people. Unfortunately, we can't fix them. A basic tenet of human psychology is that you can't change people's behaviors or actions. All you can do is change your reaction to them.

This chapter will cover some of the more typical frustrating audience responses and suggestions on how to best handle them.

Emotion

When a person is genuinely upset about something—perhaps angry at an outcome or indignant about an injustice—she may be emotional and perhaps even irrational. The worst thing you can do is ignore or discount that feeling. Try to acknowledge the emotion. That way you're more likely to diffuse it. *Hearing your experience is upsetting to me because I don't like any of our customers unhappy.* Be careful of saying, "I understand how you feel." Instead, make your understanding as specific as possible. *I'd be angry, too, if my service was cut off...* or *I don't blame you for being upset about this....*

When it's a questioner who's being emotional, it's important that you acknowledge the emotion before you even attempt to answer the question. If you don't diffuse the emotion, it won't matter what your answer is.

Monopolizing

Occasionally you may have to deal with a person who is intent on dominating the situation. This is the person who keeps hammering you, who just keeps challenging your position or harping on a particular issue. If you keep responding to this person, you'll be having an exclusive dialogue just with him. There's a two-step approach to dealing with it.

First, simply ignore the person. It's hard for someone to badger you if you don't even acknowledge his existence. If that doesn't work, it's time for step two, where you defer the issue to later. You could say, *I can see that this is important to you. But since I need to finish my presentation (or address other questions), please meet with me after the program and we can discuss it in more detail then.* The irony is, of course, that you'll probably never see the person afterward. People like that are not as interested in answers as they are in publicly venting their gripes. So take control and don't let them monopolize your session.

Hostility

When a person attacks or insults you, the key is to not get defensive. Remember that after all is said and done, what audiences remember is not so much your exact answers, but how they felt about you. Were you

Keeping Cool Under Fire

A workshop participant conveyed this compelling story. Years ago, his former employer, a utility company, was planning to build a nuclear power plant, which naturally created a great deal of controversy in the community. So the power company agreed to a public debate with some anti-nuclear activists.

The proceedings began and a utility executive was scheduled to speak first. No sooner had he arrived at the lectern than one of the anti-nuclear panelists

(continued on next page)

96

Keeping Cool... (continued)

jumped up, ran over and dumped a bucket of slimy, smelly fish remains all over the speaker.

Needless to say, this was an extremely unnerving moment. That speaker could have reacted any number of ways—run off the stage, exploded into an angry outburst of expletives and name calling, perhaps even hauled off and slugged the offender. Which, of course, is exactly what the anti-nuclear proponents were counting on. They had hoped he'd lose his cool, so they could make the utility look bad.

But the speaker disappointed them. He calmly reached into his pocket for a handkerchief, took off his glasses, wiped off his face, wiped his glasses, put his glasses back on, looked out at the audience and said politely, "May I continue?" The mood shift in the audience was palpable. Even if they were against the speaker's cause, they experienced a profound respect for his reaction. Although I'm not suggesting it changed anyone's mind, it did allow for a civil, respectful attitude toward the proceedings.

defensive? Were you antagonistic? Were you sweating bullets? It's crucial to keep your cool under fire. Stick with the issue. If you remain calm and deal with the antagonist in a patient and polite manner, you're more likely to gain the audience's sympathy and respect.

Nonresponsive

This is when an audience member sits there in a closed, defensive posture, not responding to any of your comments or humor, and refusing to be drawn out. If your audience is large, you just need to ignore this person. You can try to make eye communication once in a while, but don't go overboard in trying to connect.

Once I gave a presentation to a large group and was dismayed to see a disgruntled-looking man sitting in the middle of the second row, where I couldn't miss him. He sat during my whole presentation with his arms crossed and a bored, annoyed expression on his face, never laughing at the humorous spots, never responding to anything I asked of the audience. Although it was unnerving to see someone so obviously unhappy during my presentation, I chose not to let it bother me and directed most of my presentation to the other responsive, appreciative audience members.

Afterward, this man walked up to me, extended his hand, and said sincerely, "Barbara, that was one of the best presentations I've ever been to." Well, knock me over with a feather! So be aware that some people's body language may not be revealing their true feelings and go on faith that you're making a connection.

If, however, the audience is small, a nonresponsive member can put a damper on the whole group. Especially if your aim is to persuade the group to some action, one bump on a log can influence the others' enthusiasm for your proposal. If you've done your homework and know your audience, you probably are aware of this person's potential problem. So you might try to meet with her ahead of time to see if you can pave the way to a more receptive response.

If that doesn't work, then you could to try to meet individually with other members of the group to get their support. If such advance meetings aren't possible, then during your presentation, be sure to give the problem person the chance to express her frustrations or objections and listen to her actively (see Chapter O—Other Communication) to see if you can truly understand the nature of her resistance. If she refuses to cooperate, then still give it your best shot. Let the others in the group see that you're committed to your ideas and believe in them, even if one person doesn't seem to be.

The Know-It-All

There you are, the expert, presenting the fruits of your expertise, and someone in the audience is convinced he knows more than you do. He frequently interjects his commentary: *What I do in that situation…, What I believe works better…, I've found the best way to handle that is…."* At best, these interjections might be slightly irritating; at worst, they can be subtle attempts to undermine your knowledge. You're in an awkward situation. You can't exactly tell the offending party to keep his mouth shut. But you don't want someone sabotaging your credibility.

One good strategy here is to make an ally of the know-it-all. Beat him to the punch. After you've made a point or observation, instead of risking his interruption, you might directly address him: *Ted, since you've got experience in this area, do you have anything you'd like to add?* If he does make good points, acknowledge them. If his remarks, however, are inappropriate or wrong or unrelated to the subject, then don't let him get away with it—in a nice way. *Thanks for sharing your opinion, Ted. Some people do feel that way, but what I have found....*

Side Conversations

Invariably, if you do any amount of public speaking, you're going to have to deal with the occasional side conversation. It can be distracting and unnerving when a couple of people sitting next to each other put their heads together and whisper to each other while you're trying to talk. Here's a three-step method to deal with it.

Step 1 is to ignore the culprits. I find it helps if I say to myself, *Wow, my talk is so interesting that they're talking to each other about it!* Indeed, they might be. They might just be checking on something innocuous, and the interruption won't last very long.

If, however, the talkers seem to be going on quite a bit and it's irritating not only you, but others around them, then step 2 is dead silence. Just stop talking. You can take a sip of water or look through your notes—you don't have to stare at them. Generally the silence will make their conversation all the more obvious and they'll stop in embarrassment.

If that doesn't work—and only if the talkers are truly distracting others in the group—you can resort to step 3, which is to address the offenders directly. This may feel awkward for you, but keep in mind that if some people in the group are disturbing others, the audience will look to you, the speaker, as the person in charge, the one who needs to remedy the situation. You might say: *Sally, Bob—won't you share what's so funny with the rest of us?* or *Sally, Bob—I can't help but notice you've had a lot to talk about these last few minutes. Can it wait?* or *If it can't wait, I don't mind if you want to leave the room to discuss it.* You do this, of course, with a big smile on your face.

S

Selling

*Everyone lives by selling
something, whatever be
his right to it.*
—ROBERT LOUIS
STEVENSON

When you speak to inform an audience, all you want is for them to walk away thinking, *Gee, that was interesting, I never knew that, I learned something new.* But the objective of many presentations is to *sell*—a product, a service, an idea. When this is the case, you want *action* from your audience. You want them to *do* something—to buy the product, to sign on the dotted line, to approve your proposal, to allocate the money.

Because this is a different outcome than what you want from an informative talk, it requires a few different considerations. Here are the elements you need to keep in mind if you want to sell your audience on something.

Focus on the Audience

People will only be persuaded by what's in it for them, by what's in their best interest. Suppose you've come up with an idea for a new project to do at work and are going to pitch it to your management team. This project really excites you. It's something you would really enjoy doing. Maybe you even feel it would give you a little job security in these uncertain economic times. You're confident that you could do a good job at it, so you're hopeful you'll gain some visibility in the company.

Obviously, none of these reasons for doing the project is going to be persuasive to the management team. They want to know what's in it for them, for the company—not for you.

Sound Reasoning

You can't be very persuasive unless your reasoning is sound and the audience can accept the reasoning. In order to ensure that, you want to make certain of the following:

- Establish truthful premises. If you want to persuade a group of students to drink coffee because coffee drinkers get better grades, you're treading on dangerous ground. The premise that coffee drinkers get better grades than non-coffee drinkers has no truth to it.

- Support with evidence. If you want to persuade your group that drinking coffee is unhealthy because your father drank coffee and he was always sick, that's not valid evidence. You'd have to cite research studies and medical facts to support your claim.

- Show logical correlations. If you say that Mary drank coffee this morning and then took a nap, that may be truthful and supportable. But if you conclude that drinking coffee makes you tired, there's no logical correlation. Since caffeine is known to be a stimulant and Mary's sleepiness could be attributed to any number of causes, your conclusion isn't valid.

Motivational Appeals

Many of us claim that we make our decisions based on logic, evidence, and facts. But it's an undeniable reality that our choices actually come from a much deeper level—our feelings and motivations. It's why two different political parties can look at the same facts of a situation and come up with two differing takes on it. It's why there are thousands of different makes and models of cars on the road—we are all motivated by different interests in a car, whether it be sportiness, luxury, fuel efficiency, roominess, or safety. We make decisions based on what lights our fire.

To successfully sell an audience, you must know what their hot buttons are, then push those buttons. Your challenge is to choose the appeals

Examples of Motivational Appeals

FEELINGS

Anger	Loyalty
Appreciation	Nostalgia
Belonging	Pain
Companionship	Pride
Compassion	Reverence
Courage	Sentimentality
Curiosity	Shame
Fear	Suffering
Friendship	Sympathy
Generosity	Urgency

NEEDS

Attractiveness	Investment
Authority	Knowledge
Change	Luxury
Comfort	Money
Conformity	Power
Control	Reliability
Courtesy	Respect
Creativity	Safety
Ease	Sex Appeal
Fairness	Savings
Health	Security
Honesty	Stability
Importance	Status
Innovation	Tradition
Integrity	Winning

NEED TO AVOID

Difficulties	Loss
Expense	Stress
Guilt	Surprises
Insecurity	Trouble

most likely to motivate them. You need to appeal to their heart as well as their head.

To go back to the example about pitching a new project idea to your management team, you need to know what would motivate that group. Maybe they're a visionary group, with a track record of initiating original, innovative ideas that can set the company apart. They're not spendthrifts, but they're known to be willing to invest in a venture that has a reasonable chance of return. So your pitch is going to be more successful if you hit those hot buttons. Your proposal needs to emphasize the cutting edge nature of this project, its creativity, how it would be a groundbreaking idea that would be three steps ahead of the competition.

If, on the other hand, your management team is a more conservative group—risk-averse and more comfortable with the tried and true—then your innovative appeals would turn them off in a heartbeat. You'd be more successful with an approach that emphasized the traditional nature of this idea, how it's in keeping with the company's core business, how it's been proven to work in other venues.

I'm not saying that the facts aren't important. But it's how you interpret them and present them to your audience that will determine how successful you are in selling them. The "fact" that your idea involves a new computer system can be pitched to a visionary group as the importance of change and innovation in our increasingly technological world. But to a conservative, risk-averse audience, it may have to be sold as the need for more control and security in your information systems.

What's key here is that you need to know something about your audience. The more you know what motivates them, the more you can target your presentation to appeal to those motivations.

Visualization

This technique can well cinch the deal in a persuasive talk. Maybe the audience is not quite sure—they're still on the fence, still undecided. You can bring it all home by painting a picture for them of how things would be if they do or do not accept your proposal. Help them see the beneficial outcome of doing what you propose or the negative outcome if they don't.

Suppose you've been speaking to a group of teenagers about the dangers of drinking and driving. You might wrap up by saying:

Imagine yourself at a funeral attended by hundreds of people—your friends and family members. Everyone is crying. Your parents are so grief-stricken, they cannot talk. Everywhere, you hear mourners lamenting the loss of such a young life. The funeral is yours—because you chose to drink and then drive. You thought you could handle it, but it was the alcohol doing the thinking. You never thought this could happen to you, but getting behind the wheel after drinking sealed your fate. You just wanted to have a little fun. But your choice has not only taken your life, it has shattered the lives of all those who knew you.

Action Step

What is it you want your audience to do? Ask them for it. Challenge them to do it. Call them to some type of action or change in their thinking. And make it as easy for them to do as possible. If you want them to sign a petition for lower speed limits in your neighborhood, recognize how defeating it will be to tell them all they have to do is go down to the courthouse on a Tuesday or Thursday, between the hours of 10 A.M. and 3 P.M. and ask for a Mrs. White… You better be able to whip out that petition right then and there.

Effective Organization

Now let's organize all these elements. You still use the outline form presented in Chapter C—Content, but you need to organize the body in a very specific way if you want to be persuasive.

Action

When you want your audience to *do something*, it's called an *action* proposition. To accomplish it, you use the "four questions" approach. These are the four questions you must answer in the body of your presentation if you want to successfully sell your audience:

1. **Why?** Tell them *why* there's a need for a change, what the problem is that needs to be solved. Keep in mind that few people can be persuaded to do anything without first knowing *why* they need to do it.

2. **What?** Tell them *what* your solution is to the problem. What does it look like, what are its features, the logistics, the plan?

3. **How?** Tell them *how* your plan will solve the problem. It should be absolutely clear that your proposal would be an excellent solution to the problem.

4. **Why not?** Overcome any objections—*why* they might *not* be persuaded. Obviously you would not have to persuade your audience if they were already in favor of your proposal. The whole premise behind selling is that people have some objections that have to be overcome. You'll be more successful at dispelling those objections if you raise them yourself. If you don't, then you can bet your audience will. Once an audience member comes at you with an objection—*So just where do you think we're going to get the money to pay for this? You think it grows on trees around here?*—you're on the defensive, and that's a lot harder place to operate from. It's more effective if you bring it up yourself and then overcome it.

Let's say you want to persuade the management committee to approve a new position for your department. Here's a possible outline for this *action* objective:

I. Introduction

A. **Hook:** Perhaps you'd start out by asking your audience a question such as, *Do you know how much our department spent in overtime for the last year?* Or you could deliver a startling statement: *In the last year, we've lost one customer for every 100 orders we've filled because of delays.*

B. **Reason to listen:** *Our department is the front line to our customers, and can therefore make or break a customer relationship. The smooth functioning of our department is crucial to customer satisfaction. But when we're overworked and understaffed, our work stress translates into lost business.*

II. Body

A. **Road map:** *I'd like to propose a way to improve our department's operations and therefore retain our valued customers.*

B. **Main points:**

1. **Why?** Explain all the problems your department is having with a staff shortage—work overloads, quality problems because of the overload, order backlogs, lost business, and the cost of overtime to get all the work done.

2. **What?** Describe the new staff position you're requesting as your solution to the problem. Explain the job responsibilities, and how the new employee would fit into the existing structure of the department.

3. **How?** Outline how your proposal will solve the problem. Demonstrate how this position would alleviate the burdensome workload experienced by the department, how the person in this role could handle certain things that would eliminate overtime and prevent the backlogs and bottlenecks your area is currently suffering from.

4. **Why not?** Anticipate and overcome any objections. *Now I know there's no money in this year's budget for this position. However, this position will save money by eliminating overtime and job back-*

logs. According to the calculations of our accounting department, this savings will more than offset the extra salary cost. And the savings incurred by retaining our customers is priceless.

III. Conclusion

A. **Summary:** Reiterate the problems of staff shortage in your department and how your proposal will be an excellent solution.

(**Visualization example:** *If you do not approve this position, our staff shortage will continue to rack up excessive overtime costs. And despite our best efforts, this shortage will inevitably create missed orders and poor customer service, which means we will continue to lose unhappy customers.*)

B. **Call to action:** *I'm asking you to help make our department—and our company—more successful. I'm asking for your approval for this position.*

Additional Considerations About Selling

Sometimes you're not really out to get your audience to *do* something, but there's still an element of persuasion involved because you want to influence what they think or believe. Here are a couple of other persuasive objectives and how to approach them.

Value

Perhaps you'd like to persuade an audience that an option is a desirable choice or better than other options. You'd really like to influence their point of view on something that might be somewhat subjective—option A is *better* than option B or C. It's subjective because whether I'm going to believe one option is better than another is going to depend on what criteria you use. Is Mom's Diner a better restaurant than Joe's Eats? It depends on how you define "good" in the first place. Is it based on taste, price, atmosphere, service? The criteria for a good restaurant have to be established and agreed upon.

It's true that by persuading the audience that A is the better choice, it might mean they'll take action and select A—in other words, *do something*. But the assumption is that the audience is already going to do something—select a new vendor, go out and vote, purchase a new computer system. You simply want to influence their choice.

This kind of objective is identified as a *value* proposition. Although all the elements of persuasion apply, the difference lies in how the information is organized in the body. Your introduction and conclusion elements are still the same, but the main points of the body of your talk are best organized in three steps.

Let's say you're addressing a group of people who want to get into an exercise program—they've already decided they're going to *do* some kind of exercise. You want to persuade them that swimming is the best choice, that it's better than other options. Here are the three steps that would make up your body:

1. Establish **criteria** or "ideal" standards for your proposal. Present to the audience (or even get them to contribute) the characteristics of the ideal exercise program. For example, you might suggest the ideal program should give a good cardiovascular workout, help you lose weight, be easy on your joints, strengthen and tone all your muscles, and build strong bones.

2. **Measure** your proposal against those standards. Show how swimming fulfills those criteria.

3. **Compare** how your proposal measures up to other options. This is the powerful step. Compare your proposal with what other options have to offer, say biking, running, and yoga. If you can literally do this visually, as with the example shown, it can reinforce your point. Your proposal might not compare favorably on all the criteria, but all totaled, your choice would meet more of the criteria than the other options.

Criteria	Swimming	Biking	Running	Yoga
Aerobic	✔	✔	✔	
Lose Weight	✔	✔	✔	
Easy on Joints	✔	✔		✔
Work All Muscles	✔			✔
Strong Bones			✔	
	4	3	3	2

Swimming is the best choice.

One word of caution. Do you notice anything missing from the list of criteria? How about convenience? One of the drawbacks to swimming is that you have to have access to a pool, whereas to go running, all you have to do is step out your front door. What happens if you don't know how to swim? The ability to do the exercise is an important criterion. You can't omit obvious criteria just because they don't stack up in your favor. You just have to come up with enough standards that the pros will outweigh the cons.

Fact

Another possible persuasive objective is when you want to convince your audience that something is—or is not—true. Suppose you're talking to a group of people who want to go on a diet. You've recommended the "Skinny Minnie" system. But some members of the group have questioned whether that particular diet really works. You want to prove to them that they can lose weight on this diet. When you set out to prove that something is true or correct, it's known as a *fact* proposition.

To accomplish this objective, you can draw on three different forms of proof. You don't have to use all three—any combination, or even just one, may suffice. In the organization of your fact presentation, these proof forms would make up the main points of the body:

1. **Evidence.** Present research results, studies, or other data that support your claim. In proving this diet's integrity, you might present health and nutrition studies that document this plan's success with weight loss. You could cite surveys of people who took weight off and kept it off on this diet.

2. **Personal observation.** Something you've seen or experienced personally can be very compelling. You could tell your own story of the pounds you shed on this diet plan.

3. **Expert testimony.** A validation of your claim by other people who are acknowledged as experts can build your case. You could cite testimonials from doctors and nutritionists extolling the results of this diet plan.

The best analogy to this form of persuasion is a courtroom trial. The prosecution's objective is to prove that the defendant did it. The defense wants to prove that he didn't. Each side presents evidence, witnesses, and experts in order to prove their case to the jury.

All these different objectives can be a little confusing, especially since it's fairly easy for their elements to overlap. For example, suppose you want to persuade your company's executive team to set up a fraud hotline—an *action* proposition. You'd need to answer the four questions—why, what, how, and why not.

But in setting up the reason *why* they should establish this hotline, you might present *evidence* from the FBI or other crime agencies of the high incidence of fraud in your industry and the huge losses companies realize from it. In explaining *how* your proposal will solve the problem identifying fraud, you might cite *testimony* from certified fraud examiners about the value of fraud hotlines. Or you could convey a whistle-blower's *personal experience* with the results of calling such a hotline. You may even present some *criteria* of a good fraud protection program and *compare* how a hotline measures up.

Recognize that these components are not exclusive to just one objective. The key is first, being absolutely clear in what your objective is, and second, organizing your ideas in the best way to accomplish that objective.

In my workshops, persuasive talks give participants the hardest time. I've found that their biggest challenge is lack of a clear purpose. So state your purpose clearly. Write it down in all three ways and see which one is really what you're setting out to do:

- I want to persuade the purchasing department to buy a new photocopier. *Action.*
- In selecting a new photocopier, I want to persuade them that the Wonder Wiz duplicator is better than Crank's Copier. *Value.*
- I want to prove to them that the Wonder Wiz duplicator can generate 500 copies a minute. *Fact.*

Once your purpose is clear, your main points will be easier to identify and organize, and you'll be more persuasive.

T

Team Presentations

Your company has just made the short list of vendors who are invited to make a presentation on a major new contract. With your strong team, you're confident you have what it takes to win the business. And yet, after all comers have made their team presentations, someone else got the contract. You can't believe it. How could that have happened?

While your skills, abilities, and experience will get you on the short list, those same traits got your competitors on the list, too. It takes something else to actually win the business with a team presentation. Clients are looking not only for technical expertise, but also for trust-worthiness, commitment, and chemistry.

Team presentations present a unique challenge. By definition, a team presentation means more than one person is involved. This could create a positive synergy: The whole is greater than the sum of its parts. But it could also vividly demonstrate that you're only as strong as your weakest link. Relying on others can be a blessing when individual members are strong, but an agonizing trial when you have to carry the weight of those who aren't quite up to snuff.

Team presenters have to multi-task in their mission. They have to showcase their knowledge and experience on the subject and project confident, dynamic presentation skills. They also must exhibit a unified team front and possess a "people skills" savvy that will win the client's trust and business.

Since only you are responsible for your knowledge and experience, and since presentation skills is the subject of this whole book, this chapter will focus on those last two objectives: how to present a unified, effective team and how to exhibit strong people skills so the client will like and trust you.

Team Presentation Effectiveness

Although all the delivery and organization tips for good presentations still apply, the team presentation has some unique guidelines to consider.

Do your homework. Know the client's needs and goals and the decision makers' hot buttons.

Select the members of your team. Pick members with complementary areas of expertise, and determine how many will be on the team based on the size of your prospect's team. If the client is going to have only three people present, will you be overwhelming them if you show up with six or seven? One way to handle this dilemma is to bring all six of your different "experts," but plan on only three actually making presentations. Introduce the others to the client team, specifying their area of expertise and encouraging the client to ask them questions.

Choose the team leader. It may make sense that the leader is a high-ranking executive in your company. But consider the message you're sending if the president leads the team presentation yet will have no role in actually serving the client. It might be more meaningful if your team leader is the person who would have the most contact with the client after the sale.

Adapt to the presentation logistics. Find out ahead of time if this will be a formal, stand-up presentation, or a more informal, seated discussion approach. Will your team be seated separate from and facing your client audience? Or will you all be seated together around a table? While there may be a benefit to being seated among your prospects, keep in mind that being separated from them is not necessarily a competitive, divisive gesture. This simply gives you the opportunity to be seen, to capture the spotlight and show your stuff. Take advantage of it.

Will you be using visual aids? If so, make sure they're positioned so your audience can clearly see both you and the visuals. Find out what A/V equipment will be provided versus what you will have to bring. Always have a backup plan for your visual aids, such as printed handouts of your PowerPoint slides, in case your laptop or projector malfunctions.

Carefully consider your attire. Should it be traditional business or would a more casual business look be appropriate?

Outline the presentation. What will each person discuss? When and how long will each team member speak? What will be the leader's role in the presentation? The leader's job is typically to facilitate this whole process: get it started, make introductions, direct the flow, manage the Q&A, and finally make the sale. Here's a guideline to go by:

Team Presentation Outline

Introduction—*Leader*

  I. Hook

 II. Reason to listen

III. Team introductions

Body

  I. Road map—*Leader*

 II. Main points—*Individual team members* cover each main point

    A. Main point

      Team member A transitions to *member B*

    B. Main point

      Team member B transitions to *member C*

    C. Main point

      Team member C transitions to *member D*

    D. Main point

      Team member D transitions back to *leader*

Conclusion—*Leader*

  I. Summary

  II. Open for questions

      Leader refers questions to *appropriate team members*

      or

      Team members answer questions related to their expertise

  III. Closing statement—*Leader*

Prepare your content. Make sure you're responding to the prospect's criteria, that you meet time limits, and that each person knows his or her topic well. Obviously, highlight your strengths and the reasons why the client should select you, and also underscore your understanding of the client's needs and objectives.

Rehearse. This is invaluable for several reasons. First of all, it simply helps give all the team members a level of familiarity and comfort with their part of the presentation. Second, rehearsing ensures that you come in within your time limit (this is very important!). In addition, it will build competence in delivery skills. Use rehearsal as an opportunity for feedback and coaching (see Chapter F—Feedback). Videotape and candidly critique yourselves so each presenter appears confident and credible.

Plan for Q&A. Recognize that business is often won or lost in the Q&A session, so anticipate the questions you might get (especially the tough ones you'd rather not be asked!) and know how you're going to answer them. Assign each team member a subject area responsibility so you can avoid either everyone trying to answer at once or a long pause while everyone looks around deciding who's going to tackle it.

Look and act like a cohesive team. Remember that even when you're not presenting, you're still "on," representing your team. Project positive nonverbals throughout the whole presentation—look interested and supportive and affirming. Be careful you don't come across as bored while your teammates are talking. Resist grimacing or interrupting a team member if someone has made an incorrect statement. If a teammate does say something wrong, don't correct or chastise her immediately. At the appropriate moment, someone (ideally the team leader) can refer to the comment and "clarify" it: *I just want to clarify the time frame*

Pamela gave. While six weeks is the actual time from design to production, our experience shows it's wise to allow ten weeks for delivery. That way we have a cushion for any changes or unexpected developments that might come up.

Debrief after presentation. If you won the business, why did you? If you didn't, why not? Don't hesitate to ask the client why they made the decision they did. Request—and be prepared for—honest feedback. That's the only way you can learn how to win (again) the next time.

People Skills Savvy

Despite a client's insistence on a rational, objective decision-making process, the bottom line is they're going to select people they *like*. No matter how well you meet their criteria, if they don't *like* you, it won't matter. This quality has been covered in Chapter L—Likability, but here are a few more considerations for team presentations.

Understanding. How well do you understand not only the client's business and project needs, but their constraints, challenges, and difficulties? Be careful not to emphasize your strengths and assets to the exclusion of your client's needs. Be client-focused. If you can convey an understanding and sense of empathy with their problems and issues, you will increase your likability.

Attitude. Having a confident, can-do attitude is extremely appealing. You exhibit confidence when you answer questions knowledgeably, speak positively—*We can take care of that*—and don't put yourself down or sell yourself short. But be careful of being so confident that it borders on arrogance. Remember, your nonverbal behavior will telegraph your attitude. Watch your body language. If you're leaning back in the chair, with crossed arms and a bored look on your face, it won't matter what you say. The client will interpret it as disinterest. Make sure your nonverbals are open, relaxed, and interested. Lean forward when someone speaks to you. Make eye communication with every member on the team. Show your pleasure at this opportunity. Smile easily, have enthusiasm for the project. Clients want to work with pleasant, positive people.

Listening. Good listening skills add powerfully to your likability factor. There's a specific three-step technique to accomplish this called "active listening," which is covered in Chapter O—Other Communication. When your prospect talks about their issues, problems, and objectives, listen actively and respond appropriately. You'll make them feel understood, a powerful likability factor.

Interest. Without a doubt, being interested in others is one of the most powerful likability factors. Be careful that the focus of your presentation is not entirely on you and what you offer. While you certainly want to communicate your positive points, keep in mind that all your competitors are tooting their horns, too. What will impress the client and be more memorable is how much interest you take in them, as individuals and as a company. This starts well before that final presentation, of course. You want to take every opportunity to meet with the decision makers beforehand and show genuine interest in their business and their needs. Keep in mind that the client isn't interested in how difficult it will be for you to pull this off. But they'll be sincerely impressed if *you're* interested in *their* challenges and can offer ways to resolve their dilemmas. It's a basic fact of human relations that we're drawn to people who are interested in us.

People do business with those they like. And we tend to like those who like us. So exhibit these traits to show your commitment to a project and you'll increase your win factor.

U

Unique

With all these guidelines and rules I'm offering here about presentations, I don't want to convey the impression that I'm trying to create a collection of "Stepford Speakers." The world would be pretty boring if everyone delivered presentations the exact same way.

I've seen some compelling and enjoyable speakers who didn't follow every speaking rule. They might have stood behind a lectern instead of moving across a stage or to and from the screen, but their content was interesting and engaging. They might have been soft-spoken but spoke with such emotion and sincerity that the audience was captivated. They might have had minimal kinesics but were such great storytellers that the audience was totally absorbed. They might have had very busy, complex visuals, but because the audience was a group of scientists or other technical professionals, they loved having all the information on the screen in front of them.

All the tips I've offered in this book will undoubtedly help you be a stron-

Unique Differences

A motivational speaker needed to entertain and energize his audience. He exerted almost constant physical energy. He ran, jumped, shouted, and once climbed a platform on the stage and let out a Tarzan-like yell from the top of it!

A minister for a hospice organization spoke to a group about the physical, emotional, and spiritual considerations of (continued on next page)

Unique Differences (continued)

dying. Her delivery was soft-spoken and monotone. She didn't always speak into the microphone. But her audience was mesmerized. Everyone could relate to her topic. Her ideas were clear and compelling. And the many heart-warming and heart-breaking stories and examples she conveyed humanized the talk so much that many people were wiping away tears.

A professional speaker on business etiquette started the morning of her seminar by walking around the huge hotel ballroom and stopping at each and every attendee to shake hands and say a few words of welcome. There were 300 people in the room!

ger presenter. But the important thing to remember is that you need to *be yourself*. You have your own distinct characteristics and it's appropriate to incorporate them into your presentations. If you're a natural wit and known for your sense of humor, don't get all serious in a presentation and stifle that humor. Vice versa, if humor isn't your strong suit, then don't try to be a stand-up comedian. If you're not inherently a demonstrative person, then your audience might be a little suspicious if you start doing cartwheels across the stage. If, on the other hand, you are naturally an expressive, high-energy individual, then don't sit on your hands during your presentation. Don't try to be someone you're not.

Bring your own unique traits to your presentations. As long as you're conversational and speak to—not at—your audience, as long as your thoughts are well organized and you deliver with as much conviction as you can, you can make your own unique mark.

V

The medium is the message.
—MARSHALL McLUHAN

Visual Aids

As the old saying goes, a picture is worth a thousand words. It's well documented that when we both hear and see information, we understand it better and retain more of it. Visual aids can help achieve that in a presentation. Among their benefits, visuals can:

- Clarify your message
- Help the audience remember a point
- Generate interest
- Enhance your professionalism
- Give you purposeful movement
- Serve as your notes

But as another old saying goes, there can be too much of a good thing. There are countless problems with using visuals aids. PowerPoint, in particular, is breaking all kinds of records for the abuse and misuse of visuals. I'm going to spend most of this chapter discussing issues related to PowerPoint, although I've added some comments related to other types of visual aids at the end.

You may have purchased a CD-ROM with this book that offers PowerPoint guidelines in PowerPoint itself. If you have the CD, it would be good to review it after you've read this chapter. If you don't have it, but would like to get it, see the order form at the end of this book.

Before I get into my guidelines, let me share my overriding philosophy on visual aids: *The focus of any presentation should always be on you, the presenter.*

If your entire presentation revolves around a slide show, then why are you there? Visuals should complement and enhance your presentation, not detract from you.

I've divided my guidelines into two categories—**quality** and **usage**. If you can keep in mind that all of these are designed with this "focus on you" philosophy, I think you'll find they make a lot of sense.

Quality Guidelines

If a visual is busy or hard to read, what good is it? Here are some guidelines to help you create clean, readable visuals—ones that keep the focus on you:

1. **Follow the "UR" rule**. Like everything else about your presentation, your visuals should have a purpose. To determine how purposeful each slide is, ask yourself: Does it help the audience <u>U</u>nderstand or <u>R</u>emember my message? If not, then it's not purposeful. An example is the "title slide." This is the visual that simply states the title or name of your topic, for example: "Using Visual Aids." When you apply the "Understand or Remember" rule, you can see it does neither. So it's a useless visual. (If the audience doesn't understand or remember that you're talking about Visual Aids, then you have a bigger problem!)

   I understand the desire that many speakers have for a title slide at the beginning of their presentations. It may be necessary as a transition if you're following another speaker. It could be important for branding purposes to imprint your logo in the audience's mind. This may be appropriate. But my caution is about the use of title slides throughout your talk that serve no purpose:

   "WHAT ARE THE NEXT STEPS?"

   As a slide, this question serves no purpose. The only way it will help the audience understand or remember something is if you list the next steps.

"ADVANTAGES"
"QUESTIONS?"
"THE KEY TO SUCCESS"

These kinds of slides serve no purpose. Even transition slides, such as "STEP TWO," don't satisfy the UR rule. You don't need a visual to make transitions—*you* can be the transition. Fewer title slides means more focus on you. The alternative to the title slide, a black slide, is discussed under usage guidelines.

2. **Keep it simple.** How many times have you seen a speaker refer to his visual and say, *I know you can't read this, but...*? The more information you try to squeeze on a visual, the harder it is for the audience to read. The harder it is for them to read, the more they're going to focus on it, not you. To keep it simple, use *large type* (at least 30 pt.) and minimal wording. A good guideline is the "six by six" rule: no more than six lines per visual and no more than six words per line.

Not:

> ## Tips on Visuals
>
> - DON'T OVERWHELM YOUR VISUAL WITH TOO MUCH INFORMATION
> - THINK "BILLBOARD EFFECT" WHEN CREATING VISUALS
> - USE AT LEAST 30 PT TYPE FACE
> - NOTE THAT ALL CAPS AND SANS SERIF TYPEFACE IS HARD TO READ
> - USE NO MORE THAN SIX LINES, NO MORE THAN SIX WORDS PER LINE
> - USE PICTORIALS SUCH AS GRAPHS AND PHOTOS
> - HAVE CONTRAST IN YOUR COLOR CHOICES: LIGHT ON DARK IS MOST VISIBLE
> - STEP BACK TO THE SCREEN AND STAY WITH THE VISUAL
> - POINT, TURN, TALK - POINT TO VISUAL, TURN TO AUDIENCE AND TALK TO THEM
> - DON'T TURN OUT THE LIGHTS IN THE ROOM
> - DON'T RUN A CONTINUAL VISUAL AID SHOW

Instead:

> ## Tips on Visuals ➡ QUALITY
>
> - ✓ Keep it Simple
> - ✓ Use Large Type
> - ✓ Use Upper/Lower Case
> - ✓ Follow Six by Six Rule
> - ✓ Use Pictorials
> - ✓ Use Light on Dark Color Contrast

> ## Tips on Visuals ➡ USAGE
>
> - ✓ Step Back to Screen
> - ✓ Stay With the Visual
> - ✓ Point, Turn, Talk
> - ✓ Don't Turn Out the Lights
> - ✓ Don't Run a Continual Slide Show
>   - ➔ Insert Black Slides

You also don't need to spell out full sentences. *Use key words and phrases.*

Not: The program objectives are to revise the product to meet customer needs, while keeping development costs low to realize as high a profit as possible.

Instead: **Product Revision Objectives:**
           • Meet customer needs
           • Keep development costs low
           • Make a profit

An additional consideration is *parallelism* in your bullet points. Start each line with the same form of speech: noun, gerund (a word that ends in "ing"), or verb.

Not: ADVANTAGES
               • Improve customer service
               • Increasing productivity
               • Creates tracking system
               • Cost Savings

Instead: ADVANTAGES
               • Improves customer service
               • Increases productivity
               • Creates tracking system
               • Saves money

One final tip about readability is related to the typeface and capitalization of your text. There are two families of fonts or typefaces to choose from. **A sans serif font is plain unadorned block lettering, such as this sentence is set in. Arial and Helvetica are the two most common names of this type of font.** The second family is a **serif** typeface, such as this sentence—and most of the type in this book—is set in. Serifs are the little hooks that adorn the edges of each letter. Times New Roman and New Century Schoolbook are two common forms of serif fonts.

The basic guidelines for readability are that **serif type** is easier to read than **sans serif** and Upper/Lower Case letters are easier to read than ALL CAPS.

WHEN YOU USE ALL CAPS, ESPECIALLY IN A SANS SERIF FONT, THERE'S NO VARIATION IN THE LETTERS TO HOLD THE EYE. THIS IS DIFFICULT TO READ MORE THAN A FEW WORDS AT A TIME.

Upper and Lower Case, Especially in a Serif Typeface, Gives the Eye Something to Grab Hold of, Increasing Ease of Readability.

On your PowerPoint slides, the heading or title of the slide might do well in a sans serif type or all caps, while the text will usually be more readable in an upper- and lowercase serif font. Always make all of your text **bold.**

NEXT STEPS
- **Design the Survey**
- **Obtain the Data**
- **Analyze the Results**
- **Create Final Report**

3. **Use pictorials**. Charts, graphs, photos, and drawings used in place of, and in addition to, words can be very compelling. This is something that PowerPoint does extremely well. You can plug data into a chart and *voila!* there's a graph. Putting data, statistics, trends, or percentages into a visual form makes them much more memorable and meaningful.

Not:

- East Territory is leading with $500 millions in sales
- West Territory is a close second with sales of $400 million
- South Territory did better than last year at $300 million
- North Territory had a rough year with only $200 million

Instead:

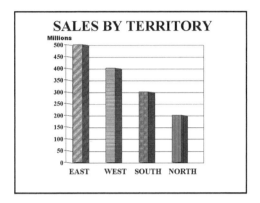

4. **Use light on dark color contrast**. Select a rich background color—dark blue or green or purple. And create all your type in either white or yellow. There are a couple of reasons for this. For starters, it's simply easier to read. As you know, light colors tend to advance and reflect, dark colors recede and absorb. A white background will reflect the light in the room more and create more of a glare. A dark background will absorb the light and recede into the background, and the light-color type will pop out of that dark background to be more readable. Second, it just looks richer and more professional. It shows your audience you cared enough to create high-quality visuals. (When you want to print these color-rich slides, just choose "black and white" or "grayscale" in your print option.)

5. **Be careful of animation.** Yes, flying bullets look neat. A background that dissolves into little diamonds is a fun effect. Sound effects, such as screeching tires or a bomb exploding, sure do sound cool. But, once again, with all that busywork with your visuals, where's the focus? Not on you. Also keep in mind that every mouse click or keystroke you have to make takes up more time. Given that most presentations usually have a time limit to them, you really don't want to do anything to unnecessarily lengthen your time. It's cleaner and simpler if you reveal your entire slide at once and talk your audience through each point on it.

I see this overuse of animation a lot in my workshops. A speaker comes in with a PowerPoint presentation for a five-minute talk.

The presentation might have ten slides (which is really pushing it for a five-minute talk). But then every slide, which has five or six bullets on it, is animated so that every line flies in at a mouse click. Do the math. That would be between 50 and 60 mouse clicks for a five-minute talk. That's a click every five seconds! Where's the focus going to be in that presentation?

For information on timed animation and slide transitions, see the following section. All of these quality guidelines are vividly demonstrated on the PowerPoint CD.

Usage Guidelines

Having to juggle using the computer keyboard and mouse, plus allowing your audience to see the screen, can be an awkward business. There are definitely some ways you can manage this process to be the most effective:

1. **Stay with the visual** while you're referring to it. Step back to the screen and put yourself in the picture. When you separate yourself from the visual—whether by standing at the lectern or the computer or off to the side—you split the audience's attention. You don't want them to have to choose between looking at you or looking at the visual. By keeping yourself in the picture, you ensure that the focus stays on you.

   There are two other good reasons for standing right beside the screen. If you stand at your laptop, there's an excellent chance that your positioning will be blocking the view of the screen for some audience members. You don't want to risk that. In addition, standing by the screen gives you a chance for purposeful movement, as you can refer to the visual and direct your audience's attention to the specific line or column you want them to focus on. But remember, don't talk to the screen. You can glance at it and refer to it, but always make sure you turn and talk to your audience.

   There is one exception to this guideline. If you've ever attended or presented at a large industry conference or convention, you're familiar with the giant-sized screen commanding the center of the stage in a convention hall. An already intimidating speaking situation, it's aggravated by the fact that the proportion of screen size to speaker height implies that the visual is more important than the speaker. Under these circumstances, you can't very well put yourself in the picture (where you'll look like a dust mote on the screen) or refer to a line that's two stories above your head.

To make the best of this situation, you'll need to pull out all the stops on your energy level to compete with the presence of such a massive visual. When you do talk about something on the screen, you can refer to it generally with a gesture, even if you can't point to one line specifically. This situation really calls for you to use your visuals purposefully. In other words, make sure there are times when you don't have a visual up. Use black slides occasionally (see guideline #6) to ensure that there are times the audience can be focused exclusively on you.

This is a good place to discuss which side of the screen you should stand on. There are two schools of thought. One school says that you should stand to the side that places your lead arm next to the visual. So, if you're right-handed, then from the audience's vantage point of facing the screen, you'd be to the visual's right. That way your right arm can easily make gestures and refer to the visual. If your lead hand isn't next to the visual, you may find yourself twisting your whole body around—and therefore turning your back on your audience—when you use it to refer to the visual.

The second school of thought, and one that I personally prefer, is to stand to the left side of the screen, where the beginning of each line and bullet point is. This serves as an appropriate anchor point to stand and bring the audience's attention to each line. However, this means your left hand will be the one you use for referring to the visual. If you're right-handed, this might be a little awkward, but it's certainly doable. The advantage to the right-hander in this position is that the right hand can hold and click the cordless mouse while the left hand refers to the screen.

2. **Use a cordless mouse.** This is a wonderful tool, allowing you to stay at the screen while you advance your slides. If the option isn't available, however, and you have to use your laptop keyboard or a mouse with a cord to advance your slides, then just remember that the simpler your visuals are—fewer mouse clicks, less information

that you can talk more about—the less you'll look like a jack-in-the-box, constantly jumping from the screen to the computer.

3. **Leave the laser pointer behind.** For those of us who love toys and gadgets, the laser pointer is almost irresistible. You hold the pen-shaped object in your hand, and with the click of a button, you can shine a pinpoint of bright red light on the screen to draw the audience's attention to a particular item. I'm sorry to disappoint you gizmo-lovers, but this device, for all its high-tech appeal, has absolutely nothing to recommend its use. I have never seen it used successfully.

There are two major problems with it:

- First of all, if your visuals are done with a good color contrast, which means the background will be a dark color, it's extremely difficult to even see that little red beam. I've seen presentations where the audience had no idea the speaker was even using a laser pointer because they never saw its light.
- Second, the very nature of its use requires the speaker to face and point to the screen. This means his back is turned to the audience and he's talking to the screen, not the people in the room.

In addition, there's the possibility that the speaker might forget to turn off the laser beam after using it, and while making gestures, end up throwing that red light all over the room.

You can be the pointer. With the exception of the large screens I mentioned earlier, the vast majority of screens are of a size that makes it very easy for the speaker herself to refer to the items on the visual.

4. **Avoid preset timed animation and slide transitions**. One of PowerPoint's many features is the ability to preset the timing for all your transitions between bullets and between slides. You can predetermine how long every bullet and every slide stays up before the next one is revealed. It doesn't have to be the same amount of time for every transition. Think you need the first bullet up for five seconds, the following one for ten seconds? You can preset it. Want one slide up for 30 seconds, another for two minutes? You can stipu-

late that. During your presentation, you can just stand back and let the program advance your bullets and slides at the rates you specified. It may seem like a great option since you don't have to worry about advancing the slides yourself. You can be free of the laptop and stay with the visual as your slides automatically move ahead.

However, it is extremely rare that this feature works well. No matter how much you practice in front of your computer screen, it's almost impossible to perfectly time your remarks in front of a group to coordinate with your transitions. You might talk faster or elaborate more than you'd planned. Someone might ask you a question that will throw off your timing. You'll invariably find that either the slide show will get ahead of you, or you'll have to pause uncomfortably waiting for the next bullet point or slide to come up.

5. **Don't turn out the lights in the room.** While the obvious advantage to a darkened room is a great-looking visual, the disadvantages outweigh it. If the room is dark, the audience can't see you—once again, you're taking the focus off of yourself. In addition, you can't see the audience. It also makes it impossible for people to take notes if they want. And there's always the risk someone will take the opportunity to catch a few Zs. Better options are to simply dim the lights slightly or to turn off lights that are directly over the screen if possible. If you've used the dark background/light type color contrast for your slides, this will make them more readable in a well-lit room.

6. **Don't run a continuous slide show.** I admit, this is my soapbox issue. How I wish I could convince legions of presenters that you don't have to have a visual up all the time. In fact, it hurts you more than it helps you, because it takes the focus off of you.

You don't need a visual up to relate an anecdote or have interaction with your audience. A visual is not necessary to set the stage or to wrap up or to signal the start of Q&A. The objective of visuals is to complement what you're saying, to help the audience understand or remember a point. If your visuals are *purposeful*, it means you won't have a visual up all the time.

PowerPoint offers a wonderful, although little-known, feature that's the perfect solution to this dilemma: the *black slide*. A black slide will make the screen go dark, which now puts the focus on you. Create a black slide (see sidebar) and then copy and paste it in your document wherever you want nothing to be on the screen. This enables you to tell that story, give that example, or make that transition without the distraction of a purposeless visual.

There's another trick that will create a dark screen. If, while you're in "Slide Show" mode, you hit the "B" key on your keyboard, your screen will go dark. When you hit it (or the mouse or the arrow or enter key) again, the visual you had darkened will come back up. (Please note that this feature works only in "Slide Show" mode.) Now, before you get all excited and think, "Great! I'll just use the 'B' key to go to blank in between some of my slides," let me offer a word of caution.

How to Create a Black Slide

- Create a new slide in "Slide View."
- Choose the "Blank" template.
- When you have the Slide View of the blank slide, go up to your toolbar and under "Format," select "Background."
- Check "Omit background graphics from master."
- Click on the drop down arrow for color selections and choose black.
- Then hit "Apply."
- Once you've created one black slide, you can copy and paste it over and over.

First of all, the thing about the "B" key is that on many laptops, when you hit it the second time to get out of the black slide, it doesn't advance to your next slide. The visual you had up before the black slide will reappear. So it's going to be awkward to have to bring up your previous slide before you can go to your next one. Second, what do you think the likelihood is that you're going to remember to hit the "B" key after certain visuals? It's risky to rely on your memory. It's much simpler to just insert a black slide when you don't want anything on the screen.

The "B" key does have its advantages, however. Its best use is for impromptu needs. Someone asks a question or makes a comment and you want to discuss the raised issue without the distraction of the visual. Hit the "B," discuss the issue, and when you're ready to go back to your visual, you can hit the "B" again and there it is.

7. **End on a black slide.** This is a nice way to end your presentation—nothing on the screen to distract from you during the Q&A session or your close. You may have noticed that PowerPoint has its own black slide that ends every slide show. It's not a bad choice, although it does have the tiny type on it that says, "End of slide show. Click to exit." Not a big deal, but I have seen speakers who, moving in front of the projector with this final slide up, had that white type run across their shirt or their face. It can be a little distracting. Put your own black slide at the end and don't exit the "Slide Show" mode until you are completely done with your presentation, ready to leave the stage. If you exit "Slide Show" before you're done, the audience has to look at the "Slide Sorter View" of your program, which is busy and distracting.

A final point about PowerPoint visuals: Make sure you can give your presentation without them. Stuff happens—light bulbs blow out, the equipment doesn't work, there's no electrical outlet to be found. Don't take up your presentation time fiddling with the equipment or bemoaning your bad luck. Go forward as if nothing's amiss. If visuals are crucial to your presentation, have hard copies on hand to distribute so that your audience will have something to refer to.

Use of Other Visual Aids
Handouts

Many times, it's appropriate to give your audience handouts that go along with your presentation. Like any A/V media, they have advantages and disadvantages. The following handout options are choices in the "Print" command of PowerPoint:

- **Slide Pages.** You can choose to print your slides. That means if you have ten slides, you'll have ten pages, exact replicas of your visual on the screen. Be sure when you select the Print option that you choose "black and white" or "grayscale." Advantages are that audience members can take detailed notes on each page if they

Visual Aids <u>Can</u>:

◆ **Clarify Your Message**
◆ **Increase Memorability**
◆ **Generate More Interest and Attention**
◆ **Give You Purposeful Movement**
◆ **Serve As Your Notes**

want, and they have a takeaway of your presentation. Disadvantages are a huge use of paper and redundancy: What is the audience supposed to look at—your screen or their slide copies?

• **Handouts.** This option allows you to print up to six mini versions of your slides on a page. Advantage: It's a more economical use of paper. Disadvantages: It limits the space available for note-taking plus also allows the audience to easily see ahead.

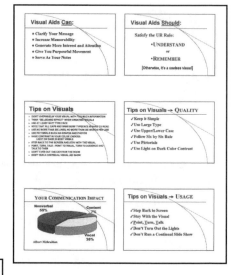

• **Outline View.** This choice allows you to print an outline of just the text from your slides. The content of several slides can go on one page. Advantages: There's a lot of white space for note taking by the audience, and it's an economical use of paper. Disadvantages: It doesn't reprint charts or graphs. And it's redundant with what's on the screen.

5 ☐ **Visual Aids <u>Can</u>:**
  ◆ Clarify Your Message
  ◆ Increase Memorability
  ◆ Generate More Interest and Attention
  ◆ Give You Purposeful Movement
  ◆ Serve As Your Notes

6 ☐ **Visual Aids <u>Should</u>:**
  Satisfy the UR Rule:
    • UNDERSTAND
    or
    • REMEMBER
  [Otherwise, it's a useless visual]

8 ☐ **Tips on Visuals → QUALITY**
  ✓ Keep it Simple
  ✓ Use Large Type
  ✓ Use Upper/Lower Case
  ✓ Follow Six by Six Rule
  ✓ Use Pictorials
  ✓ Use Light on Dark Color Contrast

10 ☐ **Tips on Visuals → USAGE**
  ✓ Step Back to Screen
  ✓ Stay With the Visual
  ✓ Point, Turn, Talk
  ✓ Don't Turn Out the Lights
  ✓ Don't Run a Continual Slide Show

- **Notes.** This prints a copy of your slide at the top and then a space at the bottom for notes. You can add your own notes, which would have more detail than the slide, or the audience can use the blank space to take their own notes. The main advantage to this is that your slide can be the simple format that uses bullet points and key words or phrases, and you can add more detailed

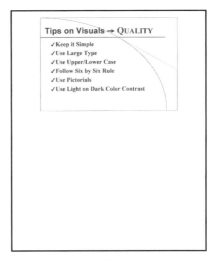

notes that will be a more complete takeaway for the audience. The disadvantages are that it's more work for you; plus it's a lot of paper since it's one slide per page.

Problems with Handouts

The main problem with Slides, Handouts, and Outline View is that you're reprinting exactly what's on your screen. If your slides are simple, as I've advocated throughout this chapter, your audience's handout will also be very simple. If they look at it a week or month later, it might not make much sense to them.

This creates a dilemma. If your visual on the screen is simple—which it should be—then your handout is probably not detailed enough to be an appropriate takeaway. But if you design your visuals so they will have more detail to beef up your handouts, then your slides will be too busy to be effective.

What I hope you'll consider is that your audience handouts don't have to be replicas of your slides. You could create a separate document that would serve as a report or summary of your presentation. When I do a workshop or presentation, that's the purpose my workbook or handout serves. My visuals may complement some of the things in my handout, but they're never exact replicas of any pages. Also, I never run a continuous slide show, but if the audience needs something to refer to, they have the notebook or handout.

My suggestion is to avoid redundancy between your slides and handouts whenever possible. Design your materials in such a way that the audience's focus will clearly be directed to either the visual or the handout (when they're not focused on you!). Let one complement the other, but avoid unnecessary duplication.

Complaints About Handouts

I hear two common complaints about handouts. One is the frustration of having the audience focus on the handout when you don't want them to. Although it's impossible to control what members of the audience do, you can minimize this by strategically choosing *when* to pass out your materials. If you hand them out *during* your presentation, then you can expect all heads to go down and focus on the handouts. One option to minimize the audience's attention on their notes is to set out the materials *ahead of time*. As members of the group come in and take their seats, they can take some time to peruse the materials before the presentation starts. That way, they've satisfied their curiosity and are more likely to focus on you when you begin. The other option is to offer them *after* your presentation. You can explain during your talk that there will be a detailed handout available afterward, so they'll be satisfied that they're getting some kind of takeaway.

The other complaint I often hear is about audience members reading ahead in the materials. This may mean they see the "punch line" before you want them to. Or they find something on page five that they'll immediately ask a question about, even though you're discussing page two. One way to minimize this is by following the previous suggestion—strategically distributing the materials either ahead of time or afterward. Another alternative is to design your handouts so they're incomplete. Put in some blanks that the audience can fill in as you go along. Purposefully leave out the key information so people won't get it before you're ready to reveal it.

Overheads

The overhead projector was once a universal staple in the world of A/V equipment. Now that PowerPoint has become so prevalent, offering much more creativity and versatility in usage and quality, the old overhead is gathering dust in many places. Still, there are a few of them left out there, valiantly supporting those speakers who use transparencies as their visual aids. So a few pointers on their use can be helpful.

- Overhead transparencies offer the advantages of ease of use and a variety of ways to prepare them. You can handwrite them, create them on the computer in a word processing program or presentation graphics program (like PowerPoint), or take existing material and photocopy it onto transparencies. You can even copy in color.
- Whatever you do, keep it readable. For example, don't photocopy a text-heavy page from a document and slap it up on your overhead. The audience will never be able to read it.
- For an element of professionalism, try to switch from one transparency to another without ever having an image off the screen. The light from the overhead projector is extremely bright and glaring, so it's more professional and easier on the audience's eyes if you can avoid having that white, empty screen staring at them. You can easily perform this maneuver using what I call the "slip and slide technique." With your right hand, "slip" the new overhead over the one already on the machine, then with your left hand "slide" the bottom one off. Do it in one fluid movement so that the screen never goes to that glaring, white blank.
- Remember to step back to the screen when referring to a visual; don't stand at the projector.
- Turn off the projector when you're not using it. If you can arrange to have your projector on a rolling cart, you can easily roll it aside when it's not in use so it's not in your way.

Flip Charts

Flip charts are great interactive media, particularly for presentations that involve lots of audience participation like brainstorming sessions and training programs.

- Anytime you can prepare the pages ahead of time, you'll save time during the presentation and ensure neater, more legible visuals.
- Use dark, but colorful markers. Yellow, orange, and pink are not readable.
- If your chart is preprepared, keep a blank sheet between pages so that the information on the next page doesn't bleed through.

- Don't place the flip chart in the center of the stage area. Remember, you want the focus on you. Place it off to one side of you, so you're in the center. The side you choose is determined by whether you're right- or left-handed and whether you're going to be doing a lot of writing on it or not.

Placement Guidelines
If you're going to be writing on your flip chart a lot:

Right-handed	Left-handed
Place the chart to your *left* side.	Place the chart to your *right*.

These placements allow you to easily turn and write with your lead hand in front of the page.

If you're going to be referring to your premade flip chart:

Right-handed	Left-handed
Place the chart to your *right*.	Place the chart to your *left*.

These placements allow you to easily refer to the visual and turn pages with your lead hand.

Props

While all the previous examples of visual aids were two-dimensional, a prop is three-dimensional. It is some kind of item that you show or demonstrate. Props can be employed symbolically, as in using an apple to represent the earth or wearing a baseball mitt to make a sports analogy. They can also be used literally, as in demonstrating how to fly fish with reel and rod in hand or walking through the steps of a recipe with the ingredients and cookware set out before you. Anyone who sells a product of some kind, whether it's makeup or cookware or clothing, is using a prop by demonstrating that product.

I've seen speakers use all kinds of props to wonderful effect: fruit, painting supplies, recipe ingredients, an umbrella, silk flowers, a model airplane. A man who talked about the story of King Kong displayed dozens of memorabilia from the movies and the book. A woman who was extolling the virtues of yoga rolled out a yoga mat and demonstrated a few yoga postures. A man in the textile business brought several samples of carpet, upholstery, and drapery for the audience to see and

Visual Aids

A Fruitful Idea

A nutritionist asked for two volunteers. She gave one an apple and one a pear and asked them to turn their fruit into a banana. When neither could obviously do it, she said, "Is there any way you can turn your apple/pear into a banana?" When she received the negative response, she turned to the audience. "Ladies, how many of you were born with a pear-shaped body?" (hands up, laughter) "How many of you were born with an apple-shaped body?" (more hands, more laughter) "Ladies, you cannot be a banana!" (Applause!)

touch. An architect unveiled a scale model of a building under construction.

Props can lend a great deal of energy and realism to your presentation. They are attention getting and engaging. They're a wonderful way to humanize your talk. Use your imagination to come up with an appropriate prop to make your point. I offer three cautionary guidelines:

- Make sure the prop is large enough for the audience to see and appreciate. Showing a vintage coin to a large group would have little impact since no one would be able to see it.

- Make sure the demonstration or operation of the prop is not so complicated that you'll have to focus too much of your attention on it instead of your audience. I once saw a speaker try to demonstrate how to pack a picnic basket. The basket had dozens of little compartments, some of which were a tight fit for some of the items. The speaker was virtually talking to the basket as she struggled to fit all the articles into it.

- If your prop is being used as a demonstration, make sure you've practiced with it enough times that your demonstration will be seamless. It's embarrassing if you have to fumble with its operation or you flip a switch and nothing happens.

Remember, visuals can enhance a presentation. They give it meaning and interest. But never sacrifice yourself for your visuals. Always keep the focus on you.

Now might be a good time to pop the PowerPoint CD into your CD drive. What better way to learn about PowerPoint issues than in a PowerPoint presentation?

W

Words for Special Occasions

Most of the tips in this book are geared toward business and professional presentations. But there are many other occasions that require you to stand up and "say a few words": wedding and anniversary toasts, funeral eulogies, awards ceremonies, acceptance speeches, dedications, and retirement tributes, to name a few. These little presentation gems call for a slightly different approach than what's been covered in this book. They may convey information, but their purpose isn't informative. They may be moving, but they don't have a persuasive objective. They simply aspire to fit the particular needs of a special occasion.

Almost every situation will be highly personalized and will require a different approach. A eulogy for your beloved grandmother would certainly be different than one for a coworker. The universal guideline is to always adapt your remarks to the audience and the occasion.

Here are some specific special occasion speeches and some guidelines to follow for them.

Toasts

A toast is a salute to a person or persons marking some special event—a wedding, anniversary, birthday—that culminates with raised glasses and a drink by all parties present. It needs to be brief, warm, and personal. Typically you toast some combination of the person or people involved, the occasion itself, and the meaning behind the event: *Here's to Jake and Sarah's 50th wedding anniversary. Their 50 years together is a testimony to their love for each other, for their children, and for life. May they have 50 more years together!*

Reciting an appropriate quote or poem could add inspiration. Wishing the celebrant(s) good health, much joy, a smooth life, or many more years of good times can also be appropriate.

The big problem with toasts is that they almost always occur in a party setting, where revelers have been drinking. I've heard some embarrassing and downright inappropriate toasts by people who had over-imbibed. So beware. If you are going to give a toast at an event, make sure you've prepared it well and that you have your wits about you when you deliver it. If you are the celebrant and want to ask someone to give the toast, choose that person with care. Your college buddy might be a good friend, but if he doesn't hold his liquor well, then you may want to choose someone else or get his commitment to observe temperance until toast time.

Awards Presentations

If you have the honor of presenting an award or other special honor to someone, the primary focus of your tribute should be on the achievements of the recipient and why he or she is receiving the award. If the audience is not familiar with the award, you may also need to explain its purpose. And if the award was won in a competition of some sort, it might be appropriate to name and praise the losers as well.

Once again, the guidelines are to be brief, warm, and personal. Your job is to make the recipient look good. So use any stories, anecdotes, or other humanizing elements that will help paint a deserving picture of the beneficiary.

Acceptance Speeches

If you've been bestowed with an award or honor, an acceptance speech is usually expected. The purpose here is to thank the organization or people who have honored you. It's also good form to recognize the people who helped you win it. A good acceptance speech is marked by three traits:

- Brevity. Our tendency is to gush effusively when we're honored. That's why the Academy Awards limits the length of acceptance speeches. Keep it short and sweet.

- Humility. This is not the time to brag. However, beware the other end of the spectrum. Complaining that you really didn't deserve this, that there are others more worthy, etc., is actually insulting to the bestowers of the award. They chose you for a reason. Honor their selection.

- Graciousness. Accept with genuine gratitude. Don't make your acceptance speech a platform for some pet peeve or political or social issue. It may be appropriate to have something positive and glowing to say about the good works of the bestowing organization.

Commemorative Speeches

A speech of praise, celebration, or inspiration is a commemorative speech. One famous example is Lincoln's Gettysburg address: "We are met on a great battlefield of that war. We have come to dedicate a portion of that field as a final resting place for those who here gave their lives that that nation might live."

Commencement addresses, building dedications, and holiday speeches are some of the examples of commemorative addresses. Their purpose is to inspire the audience, to heighten their admiration or appreciation of the person, place, or occasion. Their success lies primarily in intangible qualities, the ability to put emotions and thoughts about the occasion into words. The commemorative speaker has a challenge to use language powerfully and evocatively, to invest the occasion with dignity, meaning, and emotion.

Not all speakers are up to the challenge. But if ever presented with the opportunity, remember how important it is to come from the heart. Stay away from clichés and trite sentiment. Be dignified, sincere, and genuine.

Eulogies

This is one of the most difficult speaking assignments. To say something fitting, consoling, and inspirational about a person's life and to do so under severe emotional stress is extremely difficult. Remember how important it is to talk about the person: Praise her life and accomplishments, tell stories that reveal wonderful traits about her character, reminisce, share a favorite quote or reading of the deceased's, admit the pain of your loss and how much you miss her. Don't be afraid to relate something humorous—mourners often welcome the chance to enjoy some gentle laughter and ease their grief a little.

A funeral or memorial service is a highly personal occasion, so your remarks will be dictated by how well you knew the deceased and how well known and beloved she was to those present. The only firm guideline to observe is the old proverb, "Never speak ill of the dead."

X

eXcuses

> *Excuses change nothing, but make everyone feel better.*
>
> —MASON COOLEY

It's not uncommon when I conduct training, especially in individual coaching, that a participant is defensive and resistant to suggestions. In essence, he's saying, "Yes, but—this is the way I've always done it." We all want to cling to what's comfortable and familiar. But I challenge people to be open-minded and at least try my suggestions. (Videotaping is a powerful ally of mine—it's hard to argue with what you see on the tape.) Recognize that if you want to stand out when you stand up, you may have to go outside your comfort zone and try things you're not used to. Change isn't easy, but it's the only way to grow and improve.

Here are some of the classic excuses speakers use to justify holding on to that old, familiar way of doing things. They may be comfortable patterns, but they are not going to move you to a higher level of presentation effectiveness. Every excuse is really an illusion. See if you recognize yourself in any of these illusions. Challenge yourself to acknowledge the reality behind your illusion and implement the solution.

1. **"I just wing it."** The illusion is that you think you're better "off the cuff." But the reality is when you haven't done any preparation or are not well organized, you risk a rambling dialogue and unclear message.

    Solution: Prepare your talk. Know the main ideas you want to get across and have them coherently organized in the outline form.

2. **"This is my speech and I'm sticking to it."** This illusion believes that the speech is good just as it is regardless of the audience. The reality is that every audience is different, and if you don't relate to and adapt to their unique needs and interests, you have no chance of connecting.

   Solution: Know thy audience and relate your talk specifically to them.

3. **"I couldn't give a presentation without lots of detailed visuals."** There seem to be many people who suffer from the illusion that elaborate, complex visuals—and lots of them—will wow the audience and make them look high tech and impressive. But if you've ever been in the audience of such a speaker, you know the reality: Overdone visuals result in the medium overtaking the message and detracting from the speaker.

   Solution: Use just enough visuals to enhance your presentation, not overtake it.

4. **"I don't need visual aids—they detract from my presentation."** While it's true overdone visuals can certainly detract from the presentation, making such an unequivocal statement reveals it for the illusion it is—that visual aids are crutches that will make a presentation seem hokey. In reality, without visuals to help reinforce your main ideas, your audience might not understand or remember your points.

   Solution: Use well-done visuals to purposefully support your ideas.

5. **"I have to have notes, preferably all written out."** Do you believe the illusion that if you stick to a script, you'll be better because you won't forget anything and you'll say everything perfectly? Consider the reality. When you're over-reliant on notes, you tend to read the notes instead of deliver the ideas. This results in poor eye communication, low energy, and no connection with the audience.

   Solution: Use an outline with bullets points of your key ideas and talk to your audience—don't read to them.

6. **"The facts speak for themselves."** This illusion contends that lots of facts or statistics offer impressive evidence that validates your information. While facts are important to support your proposition, the reality is that raw, unvarnished data can be overwhelming

and meaningless without interpretation or explanation.

Solution: Humanize your talk. Make your content more interesting and memorable with anecdotes, analogies, and examples.

7. **"I have to get everything in."** Those who experience this illusion are convinced that everything they have to say on the subject is very important and audiences need to hear it all. The reality is that audiences are more interested in getting out on time. If you can't honor time constraints, you'll lose your audience.

Solution: Respect time limits. Trim your talk down to the key pearls of wisdom that will fit in the time you've been allotted.

8. **"I don't care what people think of me—I just say what has to be said."** It's great to have such a high level of confidence. But it's an illusion to believe it doesn't matter what the audience thinks just because the principle of the matter is so important. In reality, audiences don't generally respond favorably to that kind of arrogance. You can't be persuasive just from being right.

Solution: Know what motivates your audience and then appeal to those motivations. Show them what's in it for them.

9. **"I've got to be taken seriously."** This comes from the illusion that public speaking is serious business and you don't want to be construed as "silly." The tough reality to accept is that taking yourself too seriously usually results in a deadly dull presentation. If you don't smile or move or use vocal variety, you'll be a ho-hum speaker the audience will tune out.

Solution: Project energy. Use humor. Move. Gesture. Vary your vocals. Smile.

10. **"I'm not a good public speaker."** This is a very common illusion: You're panic-stricken at the prospect of addressing a group and therefore believe you'll blow it. Recognize the reality: Everyone is nervous about public speaking. But it's never killed anyone, so it's not a good enough reason to miss the crucial success-building opportunities for exposure that presentations afford.

Solution: Reading this book is a good start, of course. Get some training or coaching if you can. Practice, practice, practice. And speak often. The more you do it, the more your comfort and confidence will grow (see Chapter Y—You).

Y

You

And when things start to happen,
don't worry. Don't stew.
Just go right along.
You'll start happening too.
—THEODOR GEISEL
(DR. SEUSS)

Years ago a study was conducted on "successful" people—CEOs, presidents, business owners—those who had "arrived." The survey asked them to identify the key to their success. Their responses were divided into three categories: performance, image, and exposure—easy as PIE.

PIE

Amazingly, only 10 percent of the respondents said the key to success was **Performance**—how hard you work. Another 30 percent said the key was **Image**—your charisma, your leadership skills, how you looked, dressed, and came across to people. But the overwhelming majority, 60 percent, said the key to success was **Exposure**. In other words, it's not enough to work hard and

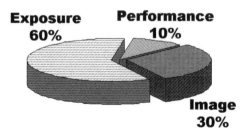

Success is as Easy as PIE

Exposure
60%
Performance
10%
Image
30%

look good if you lock yourself behind a closed door. You have to get out there and interact with your colleagues, your customers, your community.

It's a variation on that old adage, *It's who you know*. In actuality, *It's who knows you*. The more people who are exposed to your ideas, your creativity, your hard work, and your persistence, the more likely you are to be recognized and rewarded, to move up the ladder of success.

Speaking in public is a terrific way to get that exposure. In one fell swoop, you have a chance to reach many people at once and impress them with your knowledge, savvy, conviction, creativity... If you are a dynamic, compelling speaker, you can influence opinion, change minds, move people to action. You can make a difference—but only if you get out there and speak.

Get Exposure

There are a number of ways to find those opportunities for exposure.

Workplace

Start with your place of work. If your job doesn't require you to give presentations, then see if you can find a project that would give you the opportunity. Volunteer to chair some employee activity in your company such as the United Way campaign, a blood drive, or a Toys for Tots collection. These extra-curricular activities will usually require you to speak to groups of employees to enlist their support.

Organization Membership

Outside of your work, there are countless opportunities in organizations. Join professional, trade, or civic organizations and take on a visible role. If you're the treasurer, you may need to

Getting Started

During the years I was in corporate America, my job in marketing and public relations afforded me many opportunities to speak. But it wasn't until I chaired a big fund-raising event called "The Corporate Challenge" that I experienced my first speaking thrill, which cemented my love for and belief in this powerful form of communication.

On the day of the event, I found myself speaking to a crowd of hundreds of people spread out on a football field. After the first few terror-filled seconds, the adrenaline rush became a thrill. I was hooked on the excitement and power of speaking before a group.

Someone snapped my picture and I have it to this day, a memento from my first major speaking gig and a symbol of what started me on my profession of speaking and training.

report on the organization's finances at each meeting. The program chair often addresses the group to announce the upcoming meetings. And if you move up to president, you'll speak at every meeting. Volunteering for a nonprofit organization—your church, a youth group, or a social service agency—may also give you opportunities to speak.

Toastmasters

The Toastmasters organization is one of the most common venues for gaining experience in presentation skills. At Toastmasters meetings, which are usually weekly, members get opportunities to speak and evaluate other speakers. The organization has clubs everywhere, sometimes dozens in just one city. If you have any friends who are members, ask if you can come as their guest. (You might want to try more than one club, as they may have different meeting times and different personalities.) To find one on your own, go to the Toastmasters web site: www.toastmasters.org. You can enter your city to find a listing of all the clubs there. Half of all Toastmasters groups are formed in companies, so if your firm doesn't have one, you might want to spearhead that. A link on their web site tells you how.

Association Speaking

Speaking to organizations and special interest groups can be a terrific way to hone your skills and generate more exposure. Before you can go that route, though, you must know the answer to this question: *What will you talk about?*

To get speaking engagements, you have to have a topic that will be of interest and value to audiences. Generally, you have to meet one of three criteria:

1. You are an expert on a topic or subject matter that others want to learn and benefit from. A doctor who specializes in menopause issues, a karate expert, and a social worker who works with victims of domestic violence are all examples of authorities who have knowledge or expertise that audiences might be interested in.

   Look at your work—have you successfully implemented change in your organization? You might be an expert on leading change in businesses. Have you broken sales records at your company? There are tons of sales associations whose members are eager to learn selling tips. Consider your hobbies and interests. Are you a skydiver, cave spelunker, hot air balloonist, marathoner? Your knowledge and proficiency in these interesting areas could have broad appeal.

2. You've accomplished something remarkable, a feat beyond the ken of most people. Maybe you've climbed Mount Everest or hiked the entire Appalachian Trail; maybe you've had a book published or made the *Guinness Book of World Records* or won an Olympic medal. People love to hear about the exciting adventures of those who have achieved the unique or unusual.

3. You have a story to tell, one that has lessons or morals others can learn from. Examples of this are a woman who is a breast cancer survivor, an entrepreneur who started his business with nothing and became a millionaire, a woman who broke the glass ceiling in a corporation, a young man who survived a terrible car wreck but because he wasn't wearing a seat belt is now a paraplegic. If you have such a story in your life, one that might inspire and move others, this could be a great way to go.

The best places to find audiences for your talks are professional, trade, and civic associations. These groups, which usually meet monthly, are often hungry for good speakers with interesting messages. You won't get paid for these presentations, but remember, the exposure is invaluable. Ask your friends and colleagues what organizations they belong to and see if they will recommend you as a speaker to their group.

You can also do a campaign to the associations you believe would most likely benefit from your talk and offer yourself as a speaker. When I first started out in my business, I wanted to speak to as many audiences as possible as exposure for my training business. I put together a package with my bio, a brief description of the topics I could speak on, and several glowing client testimonials. I sent that to the presidents and program chairs of dozens of organizations in my community. I included a cover letter expressing my interest in speaking to their group and giving them some selling points on how my presentations could benefit their members. I didn't get a huge response, but I did have a few takers. That was all I needed to kick-start my campaign to speak as a way of marketing myself. If you can find just a couple of groups who invite you to speak, you'll find that other offers will materialize through word of mouth.

I got my mailing list for this campaign from a publication published by my local library called the "Directory of Clubs and Organizations." Check with your library to see if there's such a guide for your area. There are many other resources for finding association contacts.

- At the library, you can look up the *Encyclopedia of Associations*, a hefty volume that lists thousands of organizations.
- Another comprehensive directory you can find at the library is the *National Trade and Professional Associations of the United States*.
- Online, you can go to the Internet Public Library's directory of Associations on the Net: www.ipl.org/div/aon/. This directory provides the web addresses of thousands of associations by categories (business and economics, health and medical, law and government, etc.). You can go to those sites to get mailing addresses and phone numbers to contact their national headquarters about speaking to their local chapters or perhaps even their national conferences.
- There are also directories of associations with contact names and addresses available online for a fee. In your search engine, enter some combination of trade-professional-civic associations or organizations and browse the sites that come up to see what you can find.

Schools and Colleges

El-Hi schools (elementary through high school) love to have an expert come in and talk to students on a topic that would be interesting and valuable to them. If you have expertise in an area kids would find beneficial, this might be a great option. Do keep in mind that children are an entirely different audience than adults. You must be engaging and fun and forgiving of less-than-perfect audience members.

Most colleges have continuing education programs. These are taught by experts in the community. Analyze your knowledge and skills to see if there's a course you could teach. Continuing ed instruction can be a great option for improving your skills because courses run for a certain number of weeks. It gives you time to develop your competence and comfort level, but you don't have to make an indefinite commitment. You also get paid for your efforts!

Speaking for a Fee!

If you've mastered your delivery skills and crafted a compelling message, if audiences love your talks and give you standing ovations, then maybe you want to consider becoming a professional speaker. Imagine, being paid to talk to audiences! The goal of this book has been to help those business people who want to improve their presentation skills in their business and personal life. Professional speaking is a whole different ball game. But should you get to that point, the place to turn is the National Speakers Association: www.nsaspeaker.org. NSA is *the* resource for those who speak professionally.

Since speaking in public is an awesome form of exposure, and getting exposure is key to success, you want that exposure to be as positive and captivating as possible. That's why, in all my training workshops and throughout this book, my emphasis is always on *you*—how you can be stronger, more compelling, more dynamic, how you can stand out when you stand up.

Z

Zebra

My sister, Sharon, is a physician. She told me once about a fairly common tendency among medical students. They get excited about every unusual symptom they encounter in a patient because they believe that this will be *the one*—that serious disease, that rare disorder. But of course, the vast majority of the time, it's just a common medical ailment. In other words, they were looking and hoping for a "zebra," when it was just a plain old mule.

One of the common complaints I hear in my training business is that people believe they could be much better speakers if they didn't have to talk about dry, boring subjects. These complaints typically come from those in technical professions: engineers, scientists, accountants, actuaries, computer technicians, financial analysts, and the like. In other words, if they could talk about a zebra instead of a mule, then the topic would be much more interesting and they could do a much better job at it.

While it's true that a presentation of actuarial tables might not be as sexy as talking about a new marketing campaign, it doesn't mean you can't deliver a compelling presentation. Remember the Mehrabian research? Only 7 percent of your communication impact comes from *what you say;* but 93 percent comes from *how you look and sound* when you say it. The key is in the delivery. If you believe in what you're saying, if you have conviction and passion for your topic, then you can deliver a message that's interesting and exciting. A deadly dull presenter can't save a presentation on zebras. But an engaging, dynamic one can make even mules sound fascinating.

I have heard some fabulous presentations on some pretty dry topics. It was the speaker who made it so compelling. If you humanize your content, use your visuals effectively, and deliver with energy—if you *enjoy* yourself—then you can make any subject riveting.

So click your heels together three times and say, "There's no such thing as a dry topic. There's no such thing as a dry topic. There's no such thing as a dry topic—only a dry speaker." You have the power to make the difference!

Closing
Remarks

> *The great secret of success is that there are no secrets of success: There are only timeless principles that have proven effective throughout the centuries.*
> —BRIAN TRACY

Well, there you have it—my A to Z guide on how to stand out when you stand up. Here's a capsule of the key points from each chapter:

A. To manage **Anxiety,** prepare well, release the nervous energy through movement, lighten up, and don't forget to breathe.

B. Increase your **Believability** through your competence, your trustworthiness, and your dynamism.

C. Make your **Content** easy to understand by organizing it with the Outline Form.

D. Make your **Delivery** dynamic by smiling, projecting confident posture, making eye communication, having a professional appearance, making purposeful kinesics (gestures), having expressive vocals, and using open, relaxed resting places for your hands.

E. Put **Energy** into your presentation!

F. Learn to give and accept constructive **Feedback** to improve your skills.

G. Make speaking **Gigs** more enjoyable by enlisting the aid of a contact who will help you with all the logistics.

H. Humanize your content to make it interesting and memorable by using anecdotes, examples, analogies, humor, props, or visuals.

I. A good **Introduction** includes the speaker's name, relevant credentials, his topic and its importance to the audience, plus anything the speaker and audience have in common, and some kind of humanizing element.

J. **Jokes** are risky because there is so much that can go wrong in telling one. But humor is a great humanizing element. Sources of humor are your real life experiences, the moment, the offbeat or unexpected, cartoons.

K. **Knowledge** of your audience and your subject is crucial for credibility.

L. If you want to influence your audience, it will help if you're **Likable**. Traits of likability include being: audience-focused, confident but humble, a good listener, humorous, interested in others, upbeat, empathetic, purposeful, and not preachy.

M. If you need to use a **Microphone**, always request a lavaliere. Whether you have a lavaliere, handheld, or lectern mike, remember to do a sound check prior to speaking and always speak directly into the mike.

N. A quick reference list of presentation **No-Nos**, those pesky traits that can diminish your power and effectiveness.

O. Almost every skill that will make you a more powerful presenter will also enhance all your **Other Communication** efforts. The primary difference is your posture. When standing, a balanced, symmetrical pose has more poise. But when seated, an unbalanced asymmetrical pose is more confident. Remember that listening is a powerful communication skill and use your EAR to engage in active listening.

P. More and more presentations are conducted in the challenging venue of the **Phone Conference**. Be organized, use vocal variety, and invoke the cooperation and attention of the group.

Q. The **Q&A** session is often where you win or lose the audience's respect. Anticipate questions, use the ABC formula to answer each one, handle tough questions without getting intimidated or being trapped into negative answers, project positive nonverbals to appear poised under pressure, and always pause before answering.

R. People can be the one of the most common problems that speakers have to **Rise Above**. Keeping your cool, maintaining control, and listening actively to problem participants are some of the ways to handle difficult people.

S. The objective of many presentations is to **Sell** something—an idea, a product, a service. Incorporating the elements of persuasion and organizing your talk around your objective—action, fact, or value— will improve your chances of selling successfully.

T. **Team Presentations** present a unique challenge. Being able to present a unified, effective team and exhibit good people skills so the client will like and trust you will increase your win factor.

U. Bring your own **Unique** traits to a presentation. Be yourself.

V. **Visual Aids** have many strong benefits in presentations. By keeping them simple and readable, not overwhelming your audience with too many, and using them smoothly and professionally will help keep the focus on you, where it belongs.

W. Outside of your business and professional presentations will be opportunities to say a few **Words for Special Occasions**. Toasts, awards presentations, acceptance speeches, commemorative addresses, and eulogies are all special occasions that have special needs. Adapt your remarks to the audience and the occasion, and make them warm, moving, and inspirational.

X. A list of ten classic **eXcuses** people use that can hold them back from improving their presentations reveals them for the illusions that they are, the reality behind each illusion, and the solution to overcome them.

Y. Public speaking is an opportunity to give **You** exposure, which is a key element to success. Get out there and speak!

Z. Many speakers lament that if they had a more interesting topic, such as a **Zebra** instead of a mule, they could do a better job at presenting. But the secret is in the delivery. A deadly dull presenter can't save a presentation on zebras, but an engaging, dynamic one can make even mules sound fascinating.

Have you noticed that I organized this book the same way I recommend organizing a speech? I started with "Opening Remarks" that included a hook, a reason to listen (read), and a road map of what was covered in the book. Then each chapter, from A to Z, comprised my main points. I've just given you a summary.

So, before I close, are there any questions? ☺

In closing, I'd just like to remind you that with the power and thrill of effective speaking comes an awesome responsibility. I read somewhere that every time you speak, you are auditioning for leadership. Use your skills to improve jobs and enhance lives. Make a positive difference in the world. Be ethical, but be energetic. Be value-driven but with vitality. Be careful, but be compelling. Above all, be yourself.

May you stand out every time you stand up.

Read More About It

On Public Speaking

Carnegie, Dale. *The Quick & Easy Way to Effective Speaking.* 1962.

Drummond, Mary-Ellen. *Fearless and Flawless Public Speaking with Power, Polish, and Pizazz.* 1993.

Esposito, Janet E. *In the Spotlight: Overcome Your Fear of Public Speaking.* 2000.

Hoff, Ron. *"I Can See You Naked" A Fearless Guide to Making Great Presentations.* 1988.

Klepper, Michael M. *I'd Rather Die Than Give a Speech.* 1994.

Kushner, Malcolm. *The Light Touch—How to Use Humor for Business Success.* 1990.

Kushner, Malcolm. *Successful Presentations for Dummies.* 1996.

Kushner, Malcolm. *Public Speaking for Dummies.* 1999.

Rozakis, Laurie. *Complete Idiot's Guide to Public Speaking.* 1999.

Stevenson, Doug. *Never be Boring Again—Make Your Business Presentations Capture Attention, Inspire Action, and Produce Results.* 2003.

Walters, Lilly. *Secrets of Superstar Speakers—Wisdom from the Greatest Motivators of Our Time.* 2000.

Wilder, Lilyan. *Seven Steps to Fearless Speaking.* 1999.

Woodall, Marion K. *How to Think on Your Feet.* 1990.

Woodall, Marion K. *14 Reasons Corporate Speeches Don't Get the Job Done.* 1993.

For Humanizing Elements

Bartlett, John: *Bartlett's Familiar Quotations.* 2002 (17th edition).

Byrne, Robert. *The 2,548 Best Things Anybody Ever Said.* 2003.

Canfield, Jack, and Hansen, Mark Victor. Any of the *Chicken Soup for the Soul* series. 1990s.

Griffith, Joe. *Speaker's Library of Business—Stories, Anecdotes, and Humor.* 1990.

Panati, Charles. *Extraordinary Endings of Practically Everything and Everybody.* 1989.

Panati, Charles. *Extraordinary Origins of Everyday Things.* 1989.

Spinrad, Leonard and Thelma. *Speaker's Lifetime Library—Pithy Quotations, Witty Aphorisms, Captivating Anecdotes, Apt Comparisons, Historical Allusions, and Insightful Observations for All Occasions.* 1998.

Theibert, Philip. *How to Give a Damn Good Speech.* 1997.

Great out-loud reading for vocal inflection.

The Bells

Edgar Allen Poe

Hear the sledges with the bells—
Silver bells—
What a world of merriment their melody foretells!
How they tinkle, tinkle, tinkle,
In the icy air of night!
While the stars that oversprinkle
All the heavens, seem to twinkle
With a crystalline delight;
Keeping time, time, time,
In a sort of Runic rhyme,
To the tintinnabulation that so musically wells
From the bells, bells, bells, bells,
Bells, bells, bells—
From the jingling and the tinkling of the bells.

Hear the mellow wedding bells,
Golden bells!
What a world of happiness their harmony foretells!
Through the balmy air of night
How they ring out their delight
From the molten, golden notes!
And all in tune,
What a liquid ditty floats
To the turtle-dove that listens, while she gloats
On the moon!
Oh, from out the sounding cells,
What a gush of euphony voluminously wells:
How it swells!
How it dwells
On the Future! How it tells
Of the rapture that impels
To the swinging and the ringing
Of the bells, bells, bells—
Of the bells, bells, bells, bells,
Bells, bells, bells—
To the rhyming and the chiming of the bells!

Hear the loud alarum bells—
Brazen bells!
What a tale of terror now their turbulency tells!
In the startled ear of night
How they scream out their affright!
Too much horrified to speak,
They can only shriek, shriek,
Out of tune.
In a clamorous appealing to the mercy of the fire,
In a mad expostulation with the deaf and frantic fire,
Leaping higher, higher, higher,
With a desperate desire,
And a resolute endeavor,
Now—now to sit or never,
By the side of the pale faced moon.
Oh, the bells, bells, bells!
What a tale their terror tells
Of despair!
How they clang, and clash, and roar
What a horror they outpour
On the bosom of the palpitating air!
Yet the ear, it fully knows,
By the twanging
And the clanging,
How the danger ebbs and flows;
Yet the ear distinctly tells,
In the jangling
And the wrangling,
How the danger sinks and swells,
By the sinking or the swelling in the anger of the bells—
Of the bells—
Of the bells, bells, bells, bells,
Bells, bells, bells—
In the clamor and the clangor of the bells!

Hear the tolling of the bells—
Iron bells.
What a world of solemn thought their monody compels.
In the silence of the night
How we shiver with affright

157

At the melancholy menace of their tone.
For every sound that floats
From the rust within their throats,
Is a groan.
And the people—ah the people—
They that dwell up in the steeple
All alone,
And who tolling, tolling, tolling,
In that muffled monotone,
Feel a glory in so rolling
On the human heart a stone—
They are neither man nor woman—
They are neither brute nor human—
They are Ghouls!
And their king it is who tolls;
And he rolls, rolls, rolls, rolls,
Rolls a paean from the bells!
And his merry bosom swells
With the paean of the bells!
And he dances and he yells;
Keeping time, time, time
In a sort of Runic rhyme,
To the paean of the bells—
Of the bells;
Keeping time, time, time,
In a sort of Runic rhyme,
To the throbbing of the bells—
Of the bells, bells, bells,
To the sobbing of the bells;
Keeping time, time, time,
As he knells, knells, knells,
In a happy Runic rhyme,
To the rolling of the bells—
Of the bells, bells, bells,
To the tolling of the bells
Of the bells, bells, bells, bells,
Bells, bells, bells—
To the moaning and the groaning of the bells.

Index

Index

Give the Gift of

Stand Out When You Stand Up

to Your Friends and Colleagues

CHECK YOUR LEADING BOOKSTORE OR ORDER HERE

I would like to order:

❑ *Stand Out When You Stand Up* _____ copies at $17.95 plus
$4.95 shipping ($22.90)   _____
  North Carolina residents please add $1.26 sales tax per book   _____
  Mecklenburg County residents please add $1.35 sales tax per book   _____

❑ PowerPoint CD-ROM _____copies at $5.95 plus $2.95
shipping ($8.90)   _____
  North Carolina residents please add $ .42 sales tax per CD   _____
  Mecklenburg County residents please add $ .45 sales tax per CD   _____

❑ *The Compelling Speaker* Audio CD set _____sets at $12.95
plus $3.95 shipping ($16.90)   _____
  North Carolina residents please add $ .91 sales tax per CD set   _____
  Mecklenburg County residents please add $ .97 sales tax per CD set _____

                                          TOTAL   _____

Discounts available on quantity purchases. Please call 877-527-8210 for details.
My check or money order for $_____ is enclosed.
Please charge my: ❑ Visa ❑ MasterCard ❑ Discover ❑ American Express

Name _____

Organization _____

Address _____

City/State/Zip _____

Phone_____ E-mail _____

Card # _____

Exp. Date_____ Signature _____

Please make your check payable and return to:
Presentation Dynamics • P O Box 11713 • Charlotte, NC 28220
Call your credit card order to: 877-527-8210 / Fax: 704-522-7705
You can also order online at www.presentationdynamics.net

❑ **YES,** I am interested in having Barbara Busey speak or give a seminar to
my company, association, school, or organization. Please contact me.